The Life

Student's Book 9

New Edition

The Way, the Truth & the Life series

By Sr. Marcellina Cooney CP

Editorial Team
Angela Edwards, Martin Campion, Adam Hall, Stephen Horsman,
Ben McArdle, Rachel Smith, Mary White, Maggie Wright, Sarah Yeboah

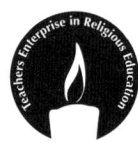

Teachers' Enterprise in Religious Education Co. Ltd

Introduction

Welcome to this edition of 'The Life' which complements 'The Way' and 'The Truth'. It is a programme of study which invites you to think deeply about what you believe, why you believe it and how it is going to help you in your journey through life. It is thought-provoking, challenging and very rewarding.

It starts with the spiritual quest, the search for God and explores not only the problem of suffering, but death, judgement, purgatory, heaven and hell. This leads on to a study of the Gospels: the life and teaching of Jesus as portrayed by each of the Evangelists with activities which relate to real-life issues.

When Jesus ascended to his Father, he gave us his Spirit. You have the opportunity to engage in an in-depth study of the gifts of the Spirit and the Sacrament of Confirmation which enables us to receive these gifts in their fullness. This leads on to the module on 'God's Call' which provides an opportunity to reflect on a variety of vocations and ways of life. Teaching about how we are to live each day is given in the module of 'Morality and Conscience'; it enables us to reflect on our actions and to come to sound decisions.

The final module 'Dialogue with Other Faiths' is important because it is only when we have a good understanding of our own faith, that we can, with confidence, share with others.

Throughout this programme, both in the Student's and Teacher's Books and on the DVD ROM, there are examples of very courageous people, who have come, frequently through great suffering, to handing over their lives to God and with His help transforming the lives of others.

My wish is that your studies this year will help you to grow closer to Jesus in faith, hope and love and that you will discover the promise his call holds for you.

✢ Vincent Nichols

✢ Vincent Nichols
Archbishop of Westminster

Contents

Introduction

1. Spiritual Quest
Search for Meaning..................................4
Searching for God....................................7
Knowing God..8
God comes to meet us............................11
The Mystery of the Trinity......................13
The Problem of Suffering.......................16
Death, Judgement, Hell, Heaven............20
Delinquent beatified...............................25
Rebel becomes inspirational Catholic..............27

2. The Gospels
Formation of the Gospels......................30
The Gospels inspired by God................32
St. Matthew's Gospel.............................33
St. Mark's Gospel...................................36
St. Luke's Gospel...................................41
St. John's Gospel...................................47
The Kingdom of God..............................49

3. Life in the Spirit
The Transforming Spirit.........................52
Gifts of the Spirit....................................54
Sacrament of Confirmation....................58
Seeds bearing fruit!................................60
Rite of the Sacrament of Confirmation..........63
Discernment..65
Pope Benedict XVI speaks to young people......67
Transformed by the Spirit......................68
Missionary in a wheelchair....................71

4. God's Call
God calls each person............................74
God's call to a specific mission.............76
What is a Vocation?................................79
Marriage..80
Sacrament of Marriage...........................82
Priesthood...86
Sacrament of Holy Orders......................88
Vocation to Religious Life.....................91
Apostolic and Monastic Religious Life............92

5. Morality & Conscience
Morality...96
Christian Morality..................................98
Current Moral Issues............................102
Conscience..106
Archbishop Romero..............................110
Irena Sendler..111
Sister Helen Prejean.............................113
Pope Benedict XVI – 'Be Saints not Celebrities'..115

6. Dialogue with Other Faiths
The Catholic Church and Other Faiths.........118
Why study Other Faiths?......................121
Types of Dialogue.................................122
Understanding Judaism........................125
Where Jews and Christians differ...............128
Understanding Islam............................130
Core Muslim beliefs.............................131
Christianity and Islam: important differences...136
Collaboration of Faith Communities............137

Glossary..142

1. Spiritual Quest

Know that each person seeks a meaning to life.
Think about what gives meaning to our lives.

Search for Meaning

Let us think about what gives meaning and purpose to our lives.

- What do I value most in life? Why?
- What is it that makes life worth living when times are difficult?
- What is it that gives me true inner peace? Why?
- Who do I treasure most? Why?

Searching in Darkness

In 1946, Viktor Frankl, a psychotherapist, wrote a book, *Man's Search for Meaning,* based on his experience with other prisoners in an Auschwitz concentration camp. He describes the reaction of all the prisoners: first, shock; then they almost gave up the will to live; some became bitter; others lost all hope and were depressed.

As Viktor spent time with the prisoners, he helped them to discover that life has meaning and it can be found even in suffering and death. When they had been forced to fast for a long period, Viktor helped each person to understand that someone was

thinking of them: a friend, family member and God. They would not want them to give up hope. He helped the prisoners to understand that in your mind you can transform situations even in severe suffering. We are spiritual beings with a God-given faith in the future. Once a prisoner lost that faith, he was doomed.

Holding on to Faith

Here is an example of how faith in the future helped the prisoners:

"We stumbled on in the darkness, over big stones and through large puddles, along the one road leading from the camp. The accompanying guards kept shouting at us and driving us with the butts of their rifles. Anyone with very sore feet supported himself on his neighbour's arm. Hardly a word was spoken; the icy wind did not encourage talk. Hiding his mouth behind his upturned collar, the man marching next to me whispered suddenly: 'If our wives could see us now! I do hope they are better off in their camps and don't know what is happening to us.'

That brought thoughts of my own wife to mind. And as we stumbled on for miles, slipping on icy spots, supporting each other time and again, dragging one another up and onward, nothing was said, but we both knew we were thinking of our wives.

Occasionally, I looked at the sky, where the stars were fading and the pink light of the morning was beginning to spread behind a dark bank of clouds. But my mind clung to my wife's image, imagining it with an uncanny acuteness. I heard her answering me; saw her smile, her frank and encouraging look. Real or not, her look was then more luminous than the sun which was beginning to rise.

A thought transfixed me: for the first time in my life I saw the truth - as it is set into song by so many poets; proclaimed as the final wisdom by so many thinkers. The truth – that love is the ultimate and the highest goal to which a person can aspire.

Then I grasped the meaning of the greatest secret that human poetry and human thought and belief have to impart: **the salvation of human beings is through love and in love.**"[1]

"Where there is no love, put love and there you will find love."

St. John of the Cross

Activities

1. a) Study the observations of Viktor Frankl.
   b) What can intense suffering do to a person?
   c) What was the great discovery that Viktor Frankl made during his time in the concentration camp?
   d) What can we learn from this discovery?

2. Look back at the questions on page 4.
   a) Think about your own personal response to those questions.
   b) Write down your responses.
   c) Share them.

3. **"Where there is no love, put love and there you will find love."**
   What do you think St. John of the Cross meant by this?
   Explain by giving an example.

4. Think of a hymn, song or a poem you know about love.
   Quote some lines from it and analyse how it helps you and may help others to focus on what is important in life.

[1] Man's search for meaning, Viktor Frankl

*Know where and how we can find God.
Reflect on our own search for God.*

Searching for God

From the earliest times, people have searched for God and this search still goes on today.

If we look closely at ourselves we will discover that there is always something we want and as soon as we get it, we want something else. We go chasing after one thing, then another and yet desire something more. As we grow up, we realise that there is always a longing and a need within us.

As a teenager, St. Augustine of Hippo lived life dangerously, expecting to find fulfilment in all kinds of pleasures. Eventually, he realised that no earthly pleasures could satisfy the deepest yearning within him. He wrote:

"You have made us for yourself O Lord, and our hearts are restless until they find rest in You".

St. Augustine had discovered that our very deepest desire, deep down within us, is for God. It is only when we recognise this and we make time for God that we will experience a profound inner peace.

Activities

1. "You have made us for yourself O Lord, and our hearts are restless until they find rest in You". St. Augustine
   - Say what **you** think about this statement and **why**.
   - Give a different point of view and say why some people hold it.
   - Explain why you disagree with them.
   - Use evidence to support your views.

2. 'The Hound of Heaven' (Worksheet TB + DVD ROM)
   Pick out difficult phrases in the poem and discuss the meaning of them.

3. a) Why do you think the poem is called 'The Hound of Heaven'?
   b) In your own words write Francis Thompson's experience as revealed in verses of the poem.
   c) Who do you think this poem is likely to help? Why?

Knowing God

How can we know that God exists?

There are three ways in which we can come to know the existence of God:
- natural reason,
- divine revelation,
- religious experience.

Natural reason

By natural reason a person can know God with certainty on the basis of His works, that is, the creation of the universe. When we see a great work of art or hear a beautiful piece of music we want to know who is responsible for it. Similarly, when we look at the world in which we live, the universe in all its complexity and beauty, we are led to ask who made it. Some theologians and philosophers have argued that only a supreme being, whom we call God, is capable of creating something so amazing.

 Study the photo on page 9.
What does it tell you about God?

Take time to reflect on some aspect of nature as you return home this evening.

If possible take a photo to share with the class.

Divine Revelation

Divine Revelation is the way in which God has gradually made Himself known to us through Abraham, Moses, David, the prophets and especially through Jesus.

In Jesus, the invisible God becomes visible.

Activity

Recall an event from the life of Abraham, Moses, David or the prophets. Explain what that event reveals about God.

(You may wish to use *The Way* or *The Truth* Books.)

Religious Experience

A very powerful way of coming to a knowledge of God's existence is through religious experience. Some people have a dramatic experience of God at work in their lives, for example, Saul on the road to Damascus. For others it is an inspiration that comes to them through other people, a time of reflection or an intense experience of beauty.

The question could be asked: how will we know that this experience is of God? We will know because such an experience will always lead to good and to a change for better in the life of the person.

Activities

1. a) Explain what happened to Saul on the road to Damascus. (Acts 9:1-19)
   b) Give reasons to explain why it was a genuine religious experience from God. Use the following references to help you:

   | 1 Cor. 13:1-7 | 1 Cor. 16:13 | 2 Cor. 4:7-11 | 2 Cor. 12:7-10 |

2. Our search for God
   To search for someone we must have an idea of who it is we are seeking.
   We find evidence of God from different sources. Slowly re-read and reflect on:
   - Natural Reason
   - Divine Revelation
   - Religious Experience

   Draw three large bubbles. In each, write a few sentences saying what you have learnt about God from each source.

3. Use a page to draw an outline of your two hands.
   a) On one hand list five consequences of living with a firm belief in God.
   b) On the other hand list the consequences of living as if God does not exist.

4. In the light of your study answer the questions on page 7.
   In small groups, share your answers.

God comes to meet us

God has given us an image, a revelation, of the unimaginable. The eternal Word of God, the Word spoken from all eternity, has taken flesh in Jesus Christ. He is not only imaginable, he has been heard, seen, watched and touched by his first companions. In their letters and Gospels, they pass on to us that message and their descriptions of that wonderful experience.

Yet, this message of his companions isn't simply from the past or simply about the past. Jesus, the one of whom they speak, is alive, risen from the dead and present today. The words of those letters and Gospels come to us with a living force, the same power or force which brought Jesus through death to life. That force is the Holy Spirit, the Spirit of the one true God. This is the most powerful way in which God has made Himself known.

The Church teaches that we know by faith that Jesus is truly God and as a man, truly human. This is a mystery that Christians have thought about for hundreds of years.

> "God loved the world so much
> that He gave His only Son,
> so that everyone who believes in him may not be lost
> but may have eternal life."(Jn. 3:16)

 Pause to reflect

Jesus is there when we are alone.
He is there when someone hurts us.
He is there when no one understands us.
He is there when our world falls apart.
He is there when we call on him.

Activities

a) Research three of the most important facts that Jesus taught us about God. Clues:

| Jn. 10:30 | Jn. 14:7 | Jn. 14:9 | 1Jn. 4:7 | 1Jn. 4:8 |

b) Explain how the facts you have chosen give meaning to your life.
c) How do you think they may help others?

11

*Know about the mystery of the Trinity.
Reflect on how the Trinity gives meaning to our lives.*

The Trinity – what does it mean?

The first year of university had started. Sam was delighted to have the opportunity to make new friends. This was the first time he found himself with students of all different faiths. As they got to know each other, the topic of Catholic faith arose.

If God is all powerful, why does He allow innocent people to suffer?

Sam, do you believe in three gods? Who are they?

Sam was confused. He was alone and could find no answers. How he wished he could go back to his RE classes in school and ask all those questions! As the days passed, he was annoyed with himself that he couldn't answer his friends' questions about his faith. Then one day, as he was passing a notice board, he saw the contact details for the Catholic Chaplain. That was his opportunity.

Fr. Tim was very understanding. He knew that some of the most challenging questions to be asked were about the problem of suffering and the Trinity. The Trinity is a wonderful mystery and a reality. Although we can never fully understand this mystery, our human minds are designed to think about it, to reflect on it and work out what we can say about it.

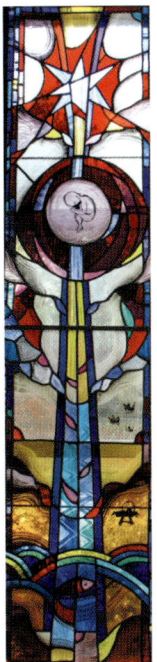

The Mystery of the Trinity

The Trinity is a mystery which can only be understood through faith. It cannot be explained like solving a mathematical problem. The Church uses metaphorical language to express the **reality** of God who is totally beyond our human grasp.

When we speak of the Trinity, that is, three 'persons' in **one God**, we are talking about the intimate life **within** God. We are speaking of the **One God** in His life of **intimate communion of love**.

It is the Father as the source of all love who surrenders Himself entirely to the Son. The Son in return surrenders himself entirely to the Father. This mutual surrendering of self is the 'SPIRIT' – love itself.

God also works outside of Himself in **creation** and **salvation**.

Creation

God, in His work outside of Himself, created the universe. He created the universe freely with wisdom and love. He created a world which is ordered and good. God does not abandon His creation but preserves and sustains it. This theological truth is revealed in the Book of Genesis in the Bible.

Salvation

We know from the Book of Genesis that human beings misused their gift of 'freedom' to turn against God their Creator. They chose to find their own self-fulfilment apart from God so sin and death entered the world. Through our ancestors, Abraham, Moses, David and the prophets, God promised us a Saviour who would free us from our sins and give us eternal life with God forever.

God in Jesus, while remaining truly God, became also truly human and came to earth to save us from sin and death.

"God loved the world so much that He sent His only Son so that everyone who believes in him may have eternal life" (Jn. 3:16).

The Spirit

After Jesus' death and resurrection and return to the 'Father', it is the **'Spirit' coming from the 'Father' and the 'Son'**, who carries **on the community of love** founded by Jesus. So the wondrous plan of God, which is to save us and the whole universe, is gradually brought to completion and fulfilment.

We know that not even the disciples who were close to Jesus understood everything he taught them. So one day, Jesus told them that he would be returning to the Father but he promised to send the Advocate, the Spirit of Truth.

**"When the Spirit of truth comes
He will lead you to the complete truth,
since he will not be speaking as from himself but
will say only what he has learnt;
and he will tell you of the things to come."** (Jn. 16:13)

a) Listen to the audio recording 'The Spirit of God'.
b) Study the written text and answer the questions. (WS TB & DVD ROM)

God is Father, Son and Spirit

When we profess our faith that this **one God** is Father, Son and Holy Spirit we are **not** referring to three 'Divine Names' given to this one God in His nature or substance. We are speaking of the **one God in His life of intimate communion of love.**

The Trinity, or Three-in-One, has been **revealed** to us by Jesus who was sent by the 'Father' out of love. He is truly and **fully God** and **fully man** (human). Because God has revealed this to us, we respond in **faith**.

14

Pause to reflect

One day, St. Augustine was walking along a beach and meditating on the Trinity. "How can God be three and one at the same time?" he kept saying over and over to himself.

Suddenly, Augustine noticed a little girl carrying a small container of water from the sea to a hole she had dug in the sand. "What are you doing?" he asked her. She replied: "I'm emptying the sea into this hole." Then it dawned on him that he was trying to do what the little girl was doing. He said to himself: "I'm trying to put the infinite God into my finite mind."

What Augustine meant was that our minds and our understanding are limited and for that reason we are unable to understand fully the infinite God; the God who is one, yet is Father, Son and Spirit.

Activities

1. The mystery of the Trinity is complex.
   a) What questions does it raise?
   b) What questions does it answer for you?

2. What part has God asked us to take in His Creation?

3. a) When and how do we receive the Holy Spirit?[2]
   b) Are we meant to feel different after it?

4. Various efforts have been made to speak about the Trinity.
   a) Study the worksheet 'The Trinity' (TB & DVD).
   b) In what ways might each example help us and why would each one be inadequate?

5. In the light of your study, write an answer to the question Sam was asked about the Trinity, page 12.

[2] *The Way*, pp. 87 and 89-91

*Know about the problem of suffering.
Reflect on the mystery of suffering*

The Problem of Suffering - why?

There are times in life when a single event unites everyone in sorrow and mourning. It has happened in Britain when a terrible accident led to the death of many children in Aberfan, South Wales. It happened in Dunblane, Scotland, when a gunman entered a primary school and shot several children and their teacher. Other events such as tsunamis and earthquakes leave us wondering where is God. Is He looking on and doing nothing? If God loves us so much how is it that He allows such disasters to take place?

Activities

Work in small groups.
a) Share your memories of disasters that you have heard about in the news.
b) Think of some of the positive things that people did at that time to support and help each other.
c) Write down some of the things you want to say to God about those events.

Cardinal Basil Hume

No matter what answers we received to the profound questions asked about suffering, they don't seem to satisfy. They leave us with further questions. Why? Why? Why?

For most of his life, Cardinal Basil Hume grappled with these baffling questions. Shortly before his death in 1999, he wrote in *The Mystery of the Cross*:

"There are no quick answers. The mystery of God is too great, and our minds too small, too limited to understand His ways. But I cannot, and will not, doubt the love of God for every person, a love that is warm, intimate and true. I shall trust Him, even when I find no human grounds for doing so. Left with the question 'Why?' I discover that a light begins to shine in the darkness, just a flicker but enough for me to say: 'I know where to look when still unable to see clearly.'

I look at the figure of Jesus dying on the cross. I know that if I look long enough, I shall begin to see that his passion and death have a powerful message to convey. When God became man, he accepted that he would be like one of us and would experience our darkest moments and greatest pain. What many humans have to endure, he endured. When many suffer the sense of being abandoned, he suffered that too. When many are troubled in mind, they know that he, too, was troubled in mind.

It's mysterious and yet what seems to be true is that God is there where we might least expect to find Him: in the massacre, the earthquake, the tsunami. Jesus underwent darkness, pain and death to give meaning to the suffering many innocent people experience. At such times, our only hold is on the Crucifix."

Pause to reflect

In 1998, Cardinal Basil Hume was not feeling well and went for a check up only to be told that he had inoperable cancer and not long to live.
He went to his private chapel and stayed for a long time before the Blessed Sacrament.
- What do you think were his thoughts?
- What do you think helped him most?
- Later, he was able to console his family and close friends who were devastated by the news. What do you think gave him the strength to do so?

The Poor in Peru

In 1985, when Pope John Paul II visited Peru, a spokesperson for the poor read this statement to him:

We are hungry
we live in misery.
We are sick and out of work.
Our infants die,
our children grow weak …
But despite this
we believe in the God of life …
We have walked
with the Church and in the Church,
and it has helped us …
to live in dignity
as children of God
and brothers and sisters of Christ.

Activities

1. Think about the above statement from the poor in Peru.
   a) Use bullet points to list the suffering they experience.
   b) How has suffering affected the lives of these people?
   c) Think of times when religious beliefs have helped people to cope with life.
   d) What can people who live in a more affluent society learn from them?

2. a) Watch the Power Point presentation of **'Mary's Meals'** and/or research the website.
   b) Analyse the information. What effect do you think it has on:
   - the founder;
   - the children;
   - the helpers;
   - and you. (www.marysmeals.org)

 **Pause to reflect**

Footprints

"One night a man had a dream. He dreamed he was walking along the beach with the LORD. Across the sky flashed scenes from his life.

For each scene, he noticed two sets of footprints in the sand; one belonging to him and the other to the LORD.

When the last scene of his life flashed before him, he looked back at the footprints in the sand.

He noticed that many times along the path of his life there was only one set of footprints. He also noticed that it happened at the very lowest and saddest times in his life.

This really bothered him and he questioned the LORD about it. 'LORD, you said that once I decided to follow you, you'd walk with me all the way. But I have noticed that during the most troublesome times in my life, there is only one set of footprints. I don't understand why, when I needed you most, you would leave me.'

The LORD replied, 'My precious, precious child, I love you and I would never leave you. During your times of trial and suffering, when you see only one set of footprints, it was then that I carried you.'"

By Mary Stephenson

- Think about the times you have been overwhelmed with problems and difficulties.
- Looking back now, what do you want to say to God?
- Take time to be alone and share your thoughts with God.

Consider what happens in death, judgement, heaven and hell. Reflect on how we can prepare now.

The Four Last Things:
Death – Judgement – Hell - Heaven

One very important truth to keep in mind is that God loves each one of us personally. From the very beginning of our existence God has taken the initiative to love us. Our part is to actively receive God's love, to become conscious of His presence and love within us and with His love to love others. Of course, we are free to close our hearts to God and not to love Him or others.

Death

If we think of the essence of life as loving God and others, then human death is not really ceasing 'to live' except in so far as our human body dies. Our soul (our real being), lives forever.

What happens when we die? This is a question that everyone has to face eventually. Dr. Elizabeth Kubler-Ross of Chicago University interviewed hundreds of people who were declared clinically dead and then revived. In general, these people all seemed to come to the following conclusions:

When you come to this point, you see that only two things are relevant: **love and the way you have treated others**. All the things we think are important like money, power, fame, prestige are of no importance.

Activities

1. What do you think is the best way to prepare for death?

2. "Look out for yourself; nobody else will."
   - Say what you **think** about this statement and **why**.
   - Give a different point of view and say why some people hold it.
   - Explain why you **disagree** with them.
   - Use evidence to support your views from:
     - findings of Dr. Elizabeth Kubler-Ross;
     - Scripture texts Luke 16:19-31 and Matthew 25:31-46;

Judgement

Our first image should be of God who took the first step to love us and always wants to love us. So think about judgement along the following lines.

- Have we opened our hearts to always receive God's love?
- Have we used God's love in us to be kind and helpful to others?
- Have we closed our hearts to God and to others – closing in on our own self-interest and self-gratification?

The Gospels tell us that there are two kinds of judgement after death:
- **Individual Judgement** at the end of each person's life on earth;
- **Last Judgement** at the end of the world.

Individual Judgement

When a person dies they experience an **Individual Judgement**. This judgement either leads to an eternal life with God or eternal separation from God.

Jesus refers to this judgement in the parable of the rich man and Lazarus. These two men, one rich, one poor, lived in the same town. The rich man had a magnificent feast every day. Lazarus, the poor man, was covered with sores and "longed to fill himself with the scraps that fell from the rich man's table. Dogs came and licked his sores.

Now the poor man died and was carried away by the angels to the bosom of Abraham. The rich man also died and was buried." (Lk. 16:21-22)

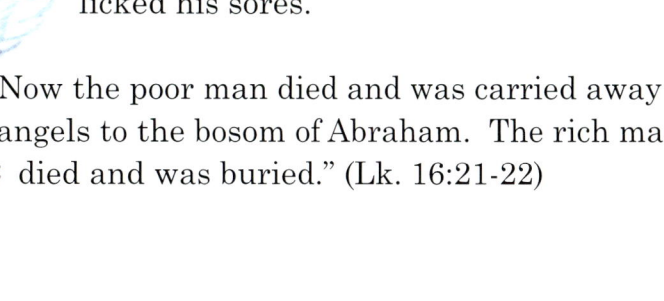

Use your Bible
a) Read the 'Parable of the rich man and Lazarus' (Lk. 16: 21-31).
b) What did the rich man experience when he died?
c) What did he beg Abraham to do?
d) What reply did he get?
e) What lesson can we learn from this parable?

Last Judgement

The Last Judgement will take place at the end of the world. The resurrection of all who have died takes place before it. At this time, all those who have done good will go on to the resurrection of life and all who have done evil will go on to the resurrection of judgement.[3] "Only God knows the day and the hour. Then through His Son, Jesus, He will pronounce the final word on all history… The Last Judgement will reveal that God's justice triumphs over all the injustices committed by His creatures and that God's love is stronger than death."[4]

Activities

1. a) Read 'The Last Judgement' (Mt. 25:31-46).
   b) What are the six criteria upon which we will be judged?
   c) Search newspapers for examples of how these criteria are being lived out today.

2. "The penalty of sin is to face, not the anger of Jesus, but the heartbreak in his eyes." William Barclay
   What do you think? Give thoughtful reasons for your answer.

[3] Cf. Catechism of the Catholic Church 1038
[4] Ibid 1040 (Abbreviated Latin *ibidem* = in the same book or passage)

Hell – what do we know about it?

When thinking of hell, let us keep in mind God who is always ready to love us. Hell is understood not as a 'place' but as a 'state' or 'condition' that a person freely chooses. This happens when a person decides that he or she does NOT want to love and does not want to be loved.

Hell is when we completely reject God and turn in on ourselves, when we become obsessed with our own needs and desires to the exclusion of everyone else. God does not punish us; we do that to ourselves by turning away from Him and inflicting suffering on others.

"The chief punishment of hell is eternal separation from God, in whom people can possess the life and happiness for which they have been created and for which they long."[5]

In Michelangelo's illustration of the Last Judgement, he has depicted people in hell as utterly miserable because they are obsessed with SELF.

Use your Bible

Read the 'Parable of the Weeds' (Mt. 13:24-30).

Scripture scholars have offered various interpretations of this parable. It is generally held that Jesus used the word *'fire'* as a metaphor, which meant burning with shame.

Whatever interpretation we put on the parable, we can be sure that God does not turn away from us but He has given us the freedom to choose.

Read the explanation of the 'Parable of the Weeds': Mt. 13:36-38
  i) What is the field?
  ii) Who is the sower?
  iii) Who are the good seeds?
  iv) Who are the weeds?
  v) When is harvest time?
  vi) Who will bring in the harvest?
  vii) What do you think Jesus wants us to understand from this parable?

[5] Catechism of the Catholic Church 1035

Purgatory - what do we know about it?

Purgatory exists because only a person completely freed from selfishness can enter into full union with God who is ALL-LOVE in heaven.

Purgatory is not a place but a 'condition'. If at the moment of earthly death there is still some selfishness in us, we need to be purified by God's 'burning love'. We must remember that after death there is no longer any 'time' or 'space'. Both of these belong to our earthly condition in this world.

 ## Pause to reflect

- What temptations encourage me to turn away from God?
- What can I do about them?
- What must I do to strengthen my relationship with God?
- Is there anyone I need to forgive?
- Do I need to ask for anyone's forgiveness?
- We can be certain that God, like the Father in the 'Parable of the Lost Son', is ever-ready to welcome us with open arms when we turn to Him for forgiveness.

Heaven - what do we know about it?

"Heaven is the endless moment of love. Nothing more separates us from God, whom our soul loves and has sought our whole life long. Together with all the angels and saints, we will be able to rejoice forever in and with God." (YOUCAT 258)

Heaven is living on in love when we are face-to-face with God. It is not a place but a state of unimaginable joy and happiness. When or if we get there, we will experience, "What no eye has seen, nor ear heard, nor the heart of man conceived, what God has prepared for those who love Him". (1 Cor. 2:9)

Activities

1. Belief in heaven gives meaning and purpose to our lives. Discuss.
   - Say what you think and why.
   - Give a different point of view and say why some people hold it.
   - Explain why you disagree with them.
   - Use evidence from the teaching of the Church to support your views.

2. Class Debate
   "Live and be merry for tomorrow we die!"
   - Is this a sound attitude to life?
   - Will it give meaning and purpose to your life?
   - Think about it from a religious and non-religious point of view.
   - Give reasons for your answer.

*Know about some people's journey of faith.
Reflect on what we can learn from them.*

Delinquent Beatified
Charles de Foucauld (1858-1916)

Charles was born in 1858 into a wealthy Catholic family in Strasbourg, France. At the age of six, he was orphaned and was brought up by his grandfather. At school he wasted his time. In fact, he was so lazy that he was expelled. By the time he was fifteen he no longer believed in God. No proof about the existence of God ever convinced him.

For a few months, Charles studied hard in order to be admitted to the military school, Saint-Cyr. He admits that at this time he was totally self-centred and full of self-love. In 1878, his grandfather died; when he received his inheritance, he spent it on self-indulgence and riotous living.

25

In 1880, his regiment was sent to Algeria and Charles took with him one of his many girl friends. However, a year later, he was dismissed from the army because of his scandalous behaviour. Some time later, he went to Morocco and got to know many Muslims. As he witnessed the Muslims practising their faith he questioned his own beliefs and began to repeat, **"My God, if you exist, let me come to know you"**.

When he returned to Paris, he took an apartment near his cousin, Marie de Bondy. He admired her intelligence but it was her deep faith in God that touched him most. He began to question his own lack of belief. He started going to church and prayed that God would make Himself known to him. Finally, God broke into his life: "The moment I knew that God existed, I knew I could not do otherwise than live for Him alone." He knew Jesus was God; nothing was more important than Jesus. He was everything.

Charles wanted to devote his life entirely to Jesus. He entered the Cistercian Trappist Order, first in France then in Syria. However he left in 1897 to lead a more solitary life of prayer. At the age of forty-three, he was ordained a priest. Then, he went to Morocco where he built a small hermitage or monastery for adoration of the Blessed Sacrament and to offer hospitality. His wish was to be a 'brother' to each and every visitor, whatever their religion, ethnic origin or social status. Later, he founded a religious order which became known as the Little Brothers of Jesus.

In 1916, Charles de Foucauld was murdered after he warned two Arab soldiers of danger from a group of rebels. He had been praying before the Blessed Sacrament when he was attacked and the rebels tossed the monstrance with the Blessed Sacrament into the sand as a useless object.

Charles de Foucauld was beatified by Pope Benedict XVI on 13 November 2005.

Activities

1. Outline Charles de Foucauld's 'Journey of Faith' using words, images and symbols.
   a) Identify key moments in his life.
   b) Explain the significance of these events.
   c) What impresses you most about his life? Why?

2. For 'Exposition' the Blessed Sacrament is placed in a monstrance. Explain to a person of another faith what is meant by the Blessed Sacrament.[6]

[6] *The Truth*, Teacher's Book, p.59

Rebel becomes Inspirational Catholic

Dorothy Day (1897-1980)

Dorothy Day's life was full of peaks and pits! She was married, but it did not work out; she found herself pregnant and had an abortion.

Nevertheless, Dorothy was always open to a sense of the Absolute; there was a God but for her He was remote. She was brought up a Protestant but did not go to church. She did read the Gospel but she did not see anyone putting it into practice.

"I did not see anyone taking off his coat and giving it to the poor. I didn't see anyone having a banquet and calling in the lame, crippled and the blind. And those who were doing it, like the Salvation Army, did not appeal to me".[7]

When she was at university, she joined a radical group who sought justice for those oppressed and found herself in prison in Washington, USA. Placed in solitary confinement, she asked for a Bible. She described her experience:

"All through those weary first days in prison when I was in solitary confinement, the only thoughts that brought comfort to my soul were those lines in the Psalm that expressed the terror and misery of people suddenly stricken and abandoned."[8]

"I lost all feeling of my own identity. I reflected on the desolation of poverty, of destitution, of sickness and sin. That I would be free after thirty days meant nothing to me.

I would never be free again, never free when I knew that behind bars all over the world there were women and men, young girls and boys, suffering constraint, punishment, isolation and hardship for crimes of which all of us were guilty."

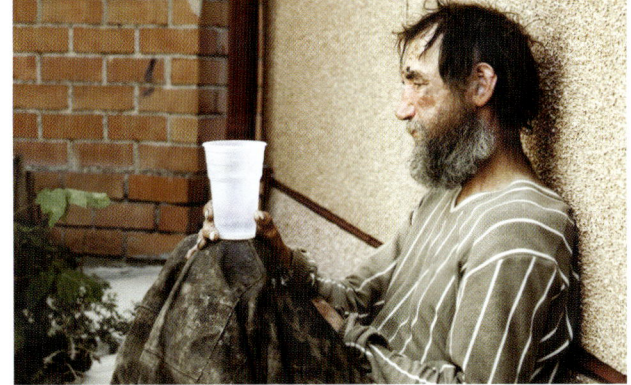

[7] The Long Loneliness
[8] From Union Square to Rome

Dorothy's faith journey

Once out of prison, Dorothy got to know some Catholic families. They reminded her of Mrs. Barrett, a Catholic whom she had known as a child. She recalls a visit to Mrs. Barrett's house:

"It was around ten o'clock in the morning that I went up to Kathryn's to call for her to come out and play. There was no one in the hall or in the kitchen. The breakfast dishes had all been washed … Thinking the children must be in the front room, I burst in and ran through the bedrooms.

In the front bedroom Mrs. Barrett was on her knees, saying her prayers. She turned to tell me that Kathryn and the children had all gone to the store and went on with her praying. I felt a burst of love toward Mrs. Barrett and I have never forgotten a feeling of gratitude and happiness that warmed my heart. She had God, and there was beauty and joy in her life.

All through my life, what she was doing remained with me… Mrs. Barrett in her little tenement flat finished her breakfast dishes at ten o'clock in the morning and got down on her knees and prayed to God."

Activities

1. The experience in prison was an important turning point in Dorothy's faith journey.
   a) She lost all feeling of her own identity. What do you think she meant?
   b) If she was going to be released from prison in thirty days, why do you think she believed she would never be free again?

2. a) Why was Mrs. Barrett so important in Dorothy's faith journey?
   b) In your opinion, who or what is most likely to support young people in their faith journey today? Give examples?

3. "There is a God-shaped vacuum in every heart." Blaise Pascal
   Suggest ways to fill it.

4. "No God, no peace. Know God, know peace." Discuss.

Dorothy describes the next stage of her faith journey

"Many a morning after sitting all night in taverns … I went to early Mass at St. Joseph's Church on Sixth Avenue. It was just around the corner from where I lived, and seeing people going to an early weekday Mass attracted me. What were they finding there? I longed for their faith. My own life was sordid and yet I had occasional glimpses of the true and the beautiful, so I used to go and kneel in the back pew of St. Joseph's."

Eventually, Dorothy became a Catholic; she said she wanted to be poor, chaste and obedient. Like all people in love, she wanted to be totally united to her loved one - Jesus. Reflecting on her past life, she was aware of her sinfulness, but she knew God was a God of love and in the Sacrament of Reconciliation she received the fullness of His grace and mercy.

Dorothy was convinced of God's continuing promise to us that He is with us always, with His comfort and joy. We only have to ask. Her Catholic faith led her and others to open 'Houses of Hospitality' across America where poor people could come for meals, clothes and accommodation. She also campaigned for improved rights for workers, and helped start the Catholic Workers Movement.

1. Imagine that Dorothy Day has been invited to be the Guest Speaker at your school Prize Giving or Speech Day.
   Some parents are concerned that she is not a good role model for young people.
   a) One parent has written a letter of complaint. Write this letter of complaint stating your objections.
   b) Write the Head Teacher's reply to the letter of complaint.

2. "With God all things are possible."
   Research:
   ◦ what Dorothy Day was able to do with God's help;
   ◦ how and where her mission continues today;
   ◦ how people can contribute to it.

2. The Gospels

*Know about the formation of the Gospels.
Reflect on what you believe about them and why you believe it.*

Formation of the Gospels

One of the most frequently discussed topics between people of different religions and faith groups is the Bible. It is very important that we have an understanding of the Gospels which tell us about the life of Jesus.

Some questions which are often asked:

Why are there four Gospels?

How can the Gospels be the Word of God when they bear the name of their authors?

If all four Gospels tell the same story why are there differences?

The Origin

The Gospels tell us of Jesus and his teaching, but they were not written by him. Jesus did not describe a miracle; he worked it. Jesus suffered and died and rose again, but he did not give an account of these events. The same is true of his teaching. His sayings and parables were spoken by him, but they were written down by others; they have come to us as others remembered them. They may have been remembered and recorded exactly as he spoke them or they may not be his exact words.

The Gospels went through three stages in reaching their final form:
- i) what the *disciples* experienced;
- ii) what the *apostles* preached;
- iii) what the *evangelists* recorded.

The Gospels were written by Matthew, Mark, Luke and John, the four evangelists. They were written some years after Jesus had risen from the dead.

Biblical experts do not all agree on the exact time and place, but in general the following is accepted.

- Matthew after 70AD in Syria
- Mark before 70AD in Rome
- Luke after 70AD in Greece
- John after 90AD in Ephesus

Why are all the Gospels different?

Let us imagine you are one of four eyewitnesses of a road accident. Each one of you is asked to produce a written statement of what happened. Which one should be taken as the correct statement?

From the written statements, the police will know that each person has witnessed the accident yet there will be variations in the reports and some similarities. This is a *little bit like* what happened with the evangelists but we must not imagine that they relied only on what they had seen or remembered. Mark was not an apostle and Luke was not even a disciple so they depended on what others told them.

Scripture experts tell us that the evangelists put the story of Jesus in writing but this story existed long before it was written. Between Jesus and the evangelists came the apostles and the early Church. When the evangelists came to write the Gospels, each one of them had a particular audience in mind:

- St. Matthew wanted to help the Jews who had converted to Christianity to understand that Jesus was the fulfilment of the Old Testament prophecies.
- St. Mark wrote mainly to help the Christians being persecuted in Rome.
- St. Luke wrote for the Gentiles (non-Jews) who wanted to become Christians.
- St. John wrote for all Christians.

Activities

1. The fact that there are four Gospels might seem problematic.
   a) What tricky questions might a Christian be asked about this fact?
   b) What answers would you give?

2. Why do the four Gospels contain different information about the same events? Do the differences invalidate them?

The Gospels inspired by God

Did God dictate to the evangelists? No. Before Jesus ascended into heaven he told the apostles what would happen:

"When the Holy Spirit comes, who reveals the truth about God, he will lead you into all the truth" (Jn. 16:12-13).

The Gospels are the inspired Word of God. In order to understand what this means, it is helpful to picture the Holy Spirit and the writer working together. Inspiration means that the Holy Spirit worked in and through the evangelists. They were empowered to use their own words and talents to communicate what God wanted them to write.

Since the Gospels are inspired, they are free from religious error; that is, free from errors related to salvation. However, it does not mean that they are free from historical or scientific errors. The document **Dei Verbum** of the Second Vatican Council states:

"Now what was handed on by the apostles includes all those things which contribute towards the holiness of life and the increase of faith of the people of God, so that the Church, in her teaching, life and worship, perpetuates and

hands on to all generations everything that she is, and everything that she believes.

The Sacred Scriptures contain the Word of God and, because they are inspired, they are truly the Word of God."

Activities

1. What does it mean when we say that the Gospels are inspired by God?
   (For help see the Catechism of the Catholic Church, para. 106; 135-136; 2 Tim. 3:16-17).

2. Work in pairs. Imagine you are with friends of another faith and they ask you the questions which are on page 30. Take turns to respond to them.

3. The quotation from **Dei Verbum** answers many questions.
   a) What are the questions?
   b) What are the answers?

Consider some events in St. Matthew's Gospel that are not covered by the other evangelists. Reflect on what they reveal about God.

St. Matthew's Gospel

While there are many similarities in the Gospels of Matthew, Mark and Luke there are some quite distinct differences which not only reveal the main intentions of the writer but some fascinating aspects of the life of Jesus. It will only be possible to touch on a few of them in this study.

Tradition identifies Matthew as the tax collector whom Jesus called to be one of his apostles. He is writing for the Christians who converted from Judaism so his main purpose is to show them that Jesus fulfils the Jewish Scriptures.

Matthew starts off with the genealogy or family tree of the Jewish people and divides it into three groups.

i) Jewish history from Abraham to David;
ii) Babylonian exile – the lowest point in the history of God's people;
iii) the birth of Jesus, the Messiah.

The genealogy lists all kinds of characters including sinners and saints. In and through these personalities, God worked out our salvation. It could be said that God was 'writing straight with crooked lines'.

Pause to discuss
Why do you think Matthew included the genealogy?

Jesus' Birth and Joseph's First Dream

St. Matthew records the birth of Jesus from Joseph's point of view. Joseph was betrothed to Mary but before they married, Mary told him that she was pregnant.

Joseph was an honest and good living man. He did not want to make an example of Mary because the punishment in those days was to stone an unfaithful woman to death. He decided to divorce her informally so as not to risk the danger of Mary being stoned to death. However, as soon as he had made up his mind, the angel of the Lord appeared to him in a dream saying:

"'Joseph, son of David, don't be afraid to take Mary as your wife, for it is by the Holy Spirit that the child has been conceived in her. She will bear a son, and you will call his name Jesus, because he will save his people from their sins'. All this took place to fulfil what the Lord has spoken by the prophet" (Mt. 1:20-22).

Activities

1. It would have been easy for Joseph to misjudge Mary.
   a) What does this text tell you about the character of Joseph?
   b) Write a short story about trust in difficult circumstances.

2. a) Read the **Visit of the Magi** (Mt. 2:1-12)
   b) What gifts did the Magi bring?
   c) Research the relevance of these gifts for later on in the life of Jesus.

3. The Magi followed the **star** that led them to Jesus.
   a) What sacrifices do you think this entailed?
   b) What qualities of character did they need?

   Follow **your** star.
   c) How will you discern the path you should follow?
   d) What qualities of character will you need to develop?
   e) What sacrifices might you have to make?

The flight into Egypt

"When the Magi had departed, an angel of the Lord appeared to Joseph in a dream and said, 'Rise, take the child and his mother, and flee to Egypt, and remain there until I tell you; for Herod is about to search for the child, to destroy him.' And he rose and took the child and his mother by night, and departed to Egypt and remained there until the death of Herod. This was to fulfil what the Lord had spoken by the prophet, 'Out of Egypt have I called my son'" (Mt. 2:13-15).

By saying, "This was to fulfil what the Lord had spoken by the prophet, 'Out of Egypt have I called my son'", Matthew is making the link with the Old Testament to show that the Jewish Scripture was being fulfilled. It also emphasised that God was in charge.

Before Jesus was able to walk or talk he was a homeless refugee. For Mary and Joseph it seemed as if their world had turned upside down. Even in situations like this, Matthew shows that the scriptures were being fulfilled.

Pause to discuss
The Childhood of Jesus
"Born as a poor deprived child? Yes!
As one that was hunted by the politically powerful because they feared he was a danger to their corrupt regime? Yes!
A baby in swaddling clothes marked for assassination? Yes!
His parents had to flee abroad as migrants and asylum seekers? Yes!"[9]

Activities

1. 'No matter what the circumstances, Joseph is obedient to God's word.'
   a) What evidence can you find to support this statement in Matthew chapters 1 and 2?
   b) How might Joseph's experiences help people who find their lives turned upside down today?

2. Identify three Old Testament prophecies mentioned in Chapters 1 and 2 of the Gospel of Matthew. To what extent have these been fulfilled?

 *Know that Mark's Gospel focuses on Jesus as the Christ and the Son of God.*
Reflect on Jesus' invitation to follow him.

St. Mark's Gospel

Mark travelled with Peter and Paul. In 64 AD, during the reign of the Emperor Nero, there was a great fire which destroyed a large area of Rome. The Emperor used the Christians as scapegoats, blaming them for the fire. He had many of them brutally killed. The Roman historian Tacitus wrote:
"These Christians were put on crosses and, at night time, burned as torches to light up the darkness".

So it was for these persecuted Christians, primarily, that Mark wrote. He focuses mainly on who Jesus is and what being a disciple involves.

[9] Fr. Shay Cullen

Who is Jesus for the disciples?

Jesus chose twelve disciples. At first, life for them was an exciting adventure. They hardly had time to eat or sleep. They felt privileged to be chosen particularly as everyone was amazed at their Master's teaching. He was seen to have great authority. He could cast out unclean spirits. He healed Simon Peter's mother-in-law. He cured the crippled and the paralysed.

> Jesus said to the paralysed man, "Get up, pick up your stretcher and walk". (Mk. 2:11)

The lame and those with highly contagious diseases all came trusting that Jesus would heal them. A leper pleaded, "If you want to you can cure me".

> Jesus stretched out his hand, touched the leper and said, "Of course I want to heal you. Be cured!"
> (Mk. 1:41)

Word soon spread about the miracles and wonders Jesus was performing. Crowds surrounded him wherever he went. Unclean spirits fell down before him and cried out saying, "You are the Son of God" (Mk. 3:7-12).

Jesus used images which everyone recognised to teach the people but they had to think deeply to grasp the meaning. Frequently, even the disciples failed to understand and Jesus had to explain it to them.

Activities

1. Work in pairs.
   Imagine you are the disciples. You are telling your friends about the miracles and teaching of Jesus. You have 60 seconds to hold them spellbound. What would you say? Use your imagination! Take one of the following references from Mark's Gospel.

   - Cure of a paralytic 2:1-12
   - Cure of a leper 1:40-45
   - A number of cures 1:32-34
   - Cure of Simon's mother-in-law 1:29-31
   - Cure of man with withered hand 3:1-6
   - Casting out an unclean spirit 1:21-27
   - Calming the storm 4:35-41
   - Daughter of Jairus 5:35-43
   - Five loaves 6:30-44
   - Who is the greatest? 9:34-37
   - Healing of the deaf man 7:31-37
   - Conditions for following Jesus 8:34-38
   - Cure of the blind man 10:46-52
   - The rich young man 10:17-22
   - Jesus walks on water 6:45-52

2. Imagine you have witnessed some of the miracles and heard Jesus teach.
   a) Reflect:
      - How are you feeling?
      - Who do you think Jesus is? Why?
      - Do you want to be a disciple? Why?
   b) Make a diary entry of your thoughts.

3. a) Read 'The Sower' (Mk 4:1-20).
      This is an example of an allegory with many shades of meaning.
   b) Use characters from the media to match the characteristics of the four places where the seeds fell.
   c) Give reasons for your choice.

Understanding Jesus

The disciples had been attracted to Jesus by his personality, his goodness, his teaching and by his miraculous powers. They had tremendous faith in him and felt important because the crowds were flocking to see their Master. Some of them even had lofty expectations and asked to be given a place of honour (Mk. 10:35-38).

One day, Jesus put them on the spot. He first asked, "Who do people say I am?" They replied, "John the Baptist, others say, Elijah or one of the prophets". Then Jesus asked the uncomfortable direct question, **"Who do you say I am?"** Peter spoke up and said to him, **"You are the Christ"**. He got it right, but did not fully understand.

Jesus went on to teach them that it was necessary for the Son of Man to suffer many things and be rejected by the elders and the high priests and the scribes and to be put to death and after three days to rise again. (Mk. 8:27-31)

These predictions were frightening! What did Jesus mean? The disciples were feeling dismayed and bewildered. Peter spoke up to reject such thoughts. But Jesus rebuked him saying, **"Get behind me, Satan! Because the way you think is not God's way but man's"**. Jesus knew what was to come. (Mk. 8:32-33)

God's ways are not our ways

The disciples wanted to be with Jesus and yet his words were very challenging as he laid down the conditions for following him:

"If anyone wants to be a follower of mine, let him renounce himself and take up his cross daily and follow me. For anyone who wants to save his life will lose it; but anyone who loses his life for my sake, and for the sake of the gospel, will save it. What gain, then, is it for a man to win the whole world and ruin his life?" (Mk. 8:34-36).

Pause to Reflect
- Peter was unable to grasp the mystery of God made man in Jesus.
- Suspecting that their master would suffer, the disciples feared for themselves.
- Most of us would want to say, 'Lord, this won't do. It doesn't make sense that you should suffer'.
- Is there a message here for us? What might it be?

The disciples are amazed, dismayed and bewildered.

Jesus listed three criteria to test if a person is genuinely his disciple or follower: **renouncing self, taking up the cross daily and following him.** In reality, however, these are **not** three criteria, but three expressions of one single criterion: **the Cross of Jesus Christ.** Jesus' Cross is **always and unfailingly** the 'handing over of self in love', that is:
- getting out of selfishness;
- surrendering oneself to God;
- with God's help loving others.

Jesus goes on to explain that those who follow him must be prepared to imitate him. He invites us to make the brave choice of a life like his, at least in our hearts. In return, our lives will have a deep meaning and purpose which will gradually unfold in the plan of God and lead to eternal life with Him.

Activities

1. Give examples to explain what Jesus asks of his disciples (Mk. 8:34-36).

2. a) Design an advert to recruit disciples. Outline the conditions based on:

   | Mk. 10:29-30 | Mk. 10:38-40 | Mk. 10:43-45 | Mk. 13:13 |

   b) Would you apply? Give thoughtful reasons for your answer.

3. In times of financial crisis, a few people's greed leaves millions in need. Write an article for the **Financial Times** to explain:
   a) what Jesus asks of all Christians;
   b) what greedy people are likely to gain by following his advice;
   c) what they are likely to lose by ignoring his teaching.

Understand that St. Luke focuses on Jesus' concern for the poor, the outcasts and the powerless.
Reflect on the message this has for us today.

St. Luke's Gospel

Luke came from Antioch in Syria and was a doctor by profession. He was a disciple of the Apostle Paul.

Luke's main concern was to portray Jesus as the Saviour, a Saviour who is full of compassion, tenderness and forgiveness, offering salvation to all. Jesus is concerned about the poor, the humble, the sinners, the outcasts and those on the margins of society. He is gentle and compassionate towards those in need and is ready to challenge anyone who promotes unjust structures and makes rules and regulations which make others powerless.

The Poor in Spirit

The first chapter in Luke's Gospel sets the scene. Mary was a young Jewish girl living in the village of Nazareth. At that time, women and girls had no status in society. They were seen as the servants of men.

Through the angel Gabriel, God intervened and broke into Mary's life.

"Mary, do not be afraid; you have won God's favour. Listen! You are to conceive and bear a son, and you must call him Jesus. He will be great and will be called Son of the Most High" (Lk. 1:32).

Mary wondered how this could happen because she was a virgin. She was assured that God and God alone would do it.

Mary is an example of the poor in spirit, those who are humble and open to receiving God. Overwhelmed with joy, Mary sang the Magnificat, her song of liberation:

"My soul glorifies the Lord,
my spirit rejoices in God my Saviour.
He looks on His servant in her lowliness;
henceforth all ages will call me blessed.

The Almighty works marvels for me.
Holy is His name!
His mercy is from age to age,
on those who fear Him" (Lk. 1:46-50).

The Shepherds (Lk. 2:15-20)

When Jesus was born, it was the shepherds in the field who first received the good news. Leaving their flocks, they hurried to the stable to see Jesus lying in a manger because there was no room for him in the inn.

This is significant because shepherds were regarded as outcasts. Due to the demands of their job, they were prevented from meeting certain requirements of the Jewish Law, such as washing before meals.

Activity

a) Use your Bible to read:

Lk. 1:26-38   Lk. 1:46-55   Lk. 2:8-17

b) Analyse each quotation to identify God's concern for the humble and lowly people.
c) What does Mary say about the princes, the proud and the rich?
d) Who do you think these people are today?

Be a Light to the Government

There is no better Gospel than Luke's to provide youth with the ammunition to challenge the false paths some people pursue when dealing with the poor, the homeless, the oppressed and those rejected by society. You can and you should, stir the conscience of those in authority and awaken them to the fact that this is a Christian country which has a duty to promote the values of Jesus Christ.

Activities

1. The context: imagine that following months of preparation for the General Election the country ended up with a coalition government. The Prime Minister is determined to win an overwhelming majority at the next election. He has the wisdom to target fourteen year olds (he knows they will be eligible to vote at the next election). He invites your class to address Parliament on what needs to be done.

   You have great loyalty to our country and for that reason you want to ensure that the Government lives and implements **the values and teaching of Jesus** as in **Luke's Gospel**.

   a) Work in small groups. Each group should address a different Government Department so that all **areas** are covered.
   b) Demonstrate how your proposals are likely to benefit the Government and the country, financially and spiritually.
   c) **Research the scripture quotes on pages 44-45 to support your views.**

   Here are the **areas** to be covered:
   - Crime and punishment;
   - Fair trade;
   - Education;
   - Healthcare;
   - Employment and tackling unemployment;
   - Defence;
   - Refugees and asylum seekers;
   - Status of women.

Use Luke's Gospel to research the values and teaching of Jesus.

Temptations
Temptations in the wilderness 4: 1-13
- What temptations might the Prime Minister face?
- What advice would you give to the Prime Minister?

Justice
The preaching of John the Baptist 3:1-14
- What advice does he give?
- To whom? Why?
- Who is it likely to help?
- Give reasons.

Encouragement
The Beatitudes 6:20-23
- Explain the meaning (for help see The Way pp. 43-44).

Complacency
Warning 6:24-26
- Explain and give examples of what is happening today.
- Warn of the danger of turning a blind eye.

The importance of Prayer

Importance of finding time to pray 5:15-16.
How to pray 11:1-4 and 11: 9-13.
Importance of sincere prayer 18: 9-14.
Praying before making a decision 6:12-13.
Praying when suffering 22: 39-44; 23:46.

- Study each example carefully.
- Explain how each example can help those in Parliament.
- Highlight the importance of prayer before making appointments and reaching decisions.
- Reflect on what MPs could do to influence the media so that good example spreads.

Danger of Riches

Hoarding Possessions 12:13-21

The rich man and Lazarus 16:19-31

Danger of riches 18:24-27

The widow's offering 21:1-4
- Explain the meaning.
- Make links with what is happening today.
- Suggest remedies to problems and how the country would benefit materially and spiritually from the example and teaching of Jesus.

Women

Women accompany Jesus 8:1-3

Concern for the widow 7:11-17

Woman who was a sinner 7:36-50

Martha and Mary 10:38-42

First witnesses to the Resurrection 24:1-12
- Research the status of women in society in the time of Jesus.
- What is the important message today?
- What would Jesus say to women today?
- What specific contribution might they make to the country if supported by Parliament?

God's Mercy

The lost sheep 15:8-10

The lost drachma 15:10

The lost son 15:11-32 (See *The Way* pp. 94-96)

The Pharisee and the publican 18:9-14
- Explain the message in the parables.
- Make links with drug addicts, alcoholics, homeless, etc.
- Suggest remedies to problems and how the country would benefit materially and spiritually from the example and teaching of Jesus.

2. **Follow up to the previous activity.**
   a) Each group makes a presentation to the class of their address to Parliament and the others grade their performance on a scale of 1-10. (10 for the best).
   b) Think of a way to use the best presentations to influence the values and beliefs of the school or local community, for example, a local radio programme in the form of a podcast, TV documentary or interview.

Know that St. John uses symbols to show the relationship Jesus has with his Father and believers. Think about our relationship with and in Jesus.

St. John's Gospel

It is widely accepted that John the Apostle wrote the fourth gospel at Ephesus. John is a theologian. He explains more deeply than the other evangelists, the divine mystery of who Jesus is and the relationship Jesus wants to have with us. He wants to show us that Jesus of Nazareth, a real, historical person, is the Messiah and truly God. The miracles are all signs which point to this truth.

The Mystery of Jesus

In order to understand the symbols and signs that John uses to unfold the mystery of who Jesus is and what he asks of us, we have to be prepared to think deeply. We have to look for meanings that are not immediately obvious.

John describes meetings that Jesus has with people. In each encounter, Jesus invites the person to move from a superficial level of just knowing him to the deeper level of discovering:
- who he is;
- how he can help each person;
- and if the person is ready to make a gift and surrender of self into the hands of God, to a total life transformation.

Nicodemus

Nicodemus, a Pharisee, who knew Jesus and was very impressed by what he had seen him do, came to him secretly at night and said:

"Rabbi, we know you are a teacher come from God; for no one can do these signs that you do, unless God is with him." Jesus answered him:
"I tell you most solemnly,
unless a man is born from above,
he cannot see the kingdom of God."

Nicodemus said, "How can a grown man be born? Can he go back into his mother's womb and be born again?" Jesus replied:
 "I tell you most solemnly,
unless a man is born through water and the Spirit,
he cannot enter the kingdom of God:
what is born of the flesh is flesh;
what is born of the Spirit is spirit" (Jn. 3:1-6).

Activities

1. a) What do you think were the motives and intentions of Nicodemus for coming to Jesus by night?
   b) What did Nicodemus have to gain or lose by doing so?

2. Jesus wants Nicodemus to move from a superficial level of knowing him to a deeper level of discovering his real identity.
   a) What does Nicodemus already know about Jesus?
   b) What is the deeper level that Jesus wants him to discover?
   c) How does the Church help us to move towards this level of understanding of Jesus? (Clue: Think about the sacraments).

3. An increasing number of secular humanists vigorously seize opportunities to undermine belief in God. Imagine some of your friends are influenced by them. Explain with reference to John 3:1-18 the implications of belief and of denying belief in God.

The 'I Am' Sayings

John uses several symbols to help us understand who Jesus is and the depth of the relationship he wants to have with those who believe in him.

Jesus has come so that we "may have life and have it to the full" (Jn. 10:10). Jesus tell us:

"I am the resurrection. If anyone believes in me, even though he dies he will live, and whoever lives and believes in me will never die" (Jn. 11:25).

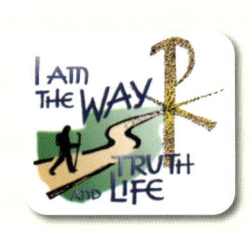

"I am the Way, the Truth and the Life. No one can come to the Father except through me. If you know me, you know my Father too" (Jn. 14:6-7).

"I am the good shepherd: the good shepherd is one who lays down his life for his sheep" (Jn. 10:11).

"I am the bread of life. He who comes to me will never be hungry; he who believes in me will never thirst" (Jn. 6:35).

"I am the light of the world; anyone who follows me will not be walking in the dark; he will have the light of life" (Jn. 8:12).

"I am the true vine, and my Father is the vine dresser ....
Whoever remains in me, with me in him, bears fruit in plenty; for cut off from me you can do nothing" (Jn. 15:1-5).

Pause to Reflect

Choose one of the sayings of Jesus. Take time to think deeply about how it might help you.

Activities

1. Work in pairs.
   Young people are constantly faced with numerous choices and challenges.
   a) Identify some of them.
   b) With reference to the sayings of Jesus, how might he be the Way, the Truth and the Life for young people?
   c) What would young people gain and what would they lose by choosing Jesus? Think on two levels: the material and the spiritual.

2. Explain the significance of Jesus, the 'Bread of Life' in the celebration of the Eucharist.[10]

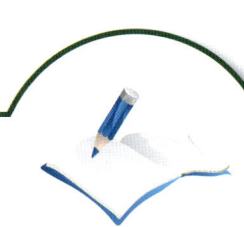

[10] *The Truth* pp. 50-52 and 60-63

*Understand that in the Gospels everyone is invited into the Kingdom of God.
Reflect on our response to this invitation.*

The Kingdom of God

"Jesus, Son of God and man, a champion of the downtrodden, one trusted and loved by the poor, the outcasts, the hungry and the sick.

Yes! And much more! He was a prophetic thorn in the side of the authorities; he challenged the injustice of his time and gave his life for his friends. He is the inspiration of young people, if they can only know him as he really was and is today."[11]

The Invitation

Jesus wants everyone to be part of his Kingdom but not everyone realises the importance of this invitation. The parable of the invited guests who made excuses, indicates what tends to happen when we are comfortable and engrossed in our own world.

Activities

1.
   a) Read Luke 14:16-24.
   b) What happened when the banquet was ready?
   c) What might represent the banquet in the life of the Church for us?
   d) What do you think is the most important message in the parable?

2. Work in pairs to find out what the Kingdom of God is like.
   a) Read: Mk. 4:30-32   Lk. 13:21   Mt. 13:44-46
   b) Match the parable with the following meanings:
      (i) When we discover the treasures that God offers us, we realise they are worth more than anything else.
      (ii) God's Kingdom starts in a small way within us and spreads until Jesus is the King of our whole life.
      (iii) The Kingdom starts small but grows quietly and powerfully until it changes us completely.

3. Look back at what you have studied in this unit.
   a) Design your own way of portraying the Kingdom of God.
   b) How could you encourage others to seek it?
   c) Explain how one can be a true witness to the Kingdom.

[11] Fr. Shay Cullen

The Kingdom is for everyone

Jesus' burning desire is to lead every single person to the Father:

"I have come
that they may have life
and have it to the full." (Jn. 10:10)

"If anyone loves me he will keep my word,
and my Father will love him,
and we shall come to him
and make our home with him." (Jn. 14:23)

The love Jesus has for each of us is boundless. He was prepared to give his life for us. No matter what we have done wrong, he is there waiting for us to turn to him for forgiveness. Like the father of the prodigal son he waits and waits, watching for us to take that step to come to him. The way is open night and day for sinners who repent and seek forgiveness.

Jesus forgives the adulterous woman.
Jn. 8:1-11

Jesus prays for those who crucify him.
Lk. 23:34

Jesus takes the thief to heaven.
Lk. 23:43

Activities

1. Imagine a situation where someone has made a serious mistake in his or her life.
   a) Give a brief outline of the situation.
   b) How might the text on this page help the person to understand that forgiveness, love and a life full of hope is possible.

2. Jesus' life-changing values are centred on a relationship of love, trust and forgiveness. The sacraments give us the grace to be witnesses of God's Kingdom and to lead others to Jesus.
   a) Which sacrament enables us to become a member of the Church?
   b) What happens when we receive this sacrament?
   c) How does it prepare us for the Kingdom of God?[12]

[12] *The Way* pp. 89-92

Has the Kingdom of God come?

Jesus explained the tension between the present time and the final coming of the Kingdom in parables and stories. Think about the parable of the Mustard Seed (Mk. 4:30-32). In it the Kingdom is compared to the tiny seed. The Kingdom came in Jesus' time on earth and yet its fulfilment will be in his second coming. The presence of God's Kingdom is here now and makes itself felt:

- whenever people forgive those who have injured them;
- wherever love and care overcome fear of one another;
- wherever the hungry are fed, the thirsty given a cup of water, the naked clothed, the homeless housed and prisoners are visited.

Has the Kingdom of God come and if so, how will we recognise it?

Reflection with Jesus

Our Father in heaven

We are your people, the work of your hands,

we praise your greatness,

we celebrate your goodness,

we remember the story of your love.

We pray that your Kingdom may come

so that it may free us from fear and darkness.

So that it may heal our brokenness

and bring peace to your creation.

Give us wisdom to understand your will and your presence

especially when we are hurt by the unexpected,

when we search for meaning in the midst of our losses,

when we are trapped by our emotions.

Give us confidence to thank your for your daily gifts we so often take for granted:

the gift of food that provides nourishment for our bodies,

the gift of beauty that provides nourishment for our minds,

the gift of love that provides nourishment for our spirits,

the gift of faith that sustains us,

the gift of friends that comforts us,

the gift of every colour in your creation that brightens our day.

Help us to forgive each other as you forgive us:

you cleanse away our resistance

and bring your light into our sleepy souls.

Help us to reach out to others,

to become healing instruments in your world,

to build bridges rather than walls in your creation. Amen.[13]

---

[13] *Throw Fire* p. 336 John Fuellenbach, SVD

3. Life in the Spirit

Know how the Holy Spirit transformed the lives of the Apostles. Appreciate that the Spirit can help us.

The Transforming Spirit

At the crucifixion, the apostles ran away and went into hiding. Only John remained at the foot of the cross.

Yet, when all seemed lost, Jesus was actually triumphing over the power of evil. The most sensational news the apostles had ever heard was that Jesus was ALIVE. Jesus had risen from the dead.

The resurrection of Jesus broke the power of sin. Just as death was not the end for Jesus, it would no longer be the end for the apostles or for us.

For forty days after the resurrection, Jesus stayed on earth. Several times, he appeared to his apostles before returning to his Father in heaven. He warned them that they would be brought before governors and kings to be tried as enemies for doing his work. They must expect to be imprisoned, beaten and even killed but the work would go on and nothing would stop it. Jesus would always be with them, even to the end of the world. More than that, Jesus would send his Spirit to be with them and give them the strength to be his witnesses everywhere. With Mary, the apostles went to the Upper Room to spend time in prayer and reflection.

The descent of the Holy Spirit

Use your Bible to read Acts 2:1-13.

When the Holy Spirit descended on the apostles, they immediately felt brave, strong and ready for anything. Now they understood what Jesus had taught them and rushed to spread the Good News.

No matter what nationality they were, all the people were able to understand the apostles speaking in their own language.

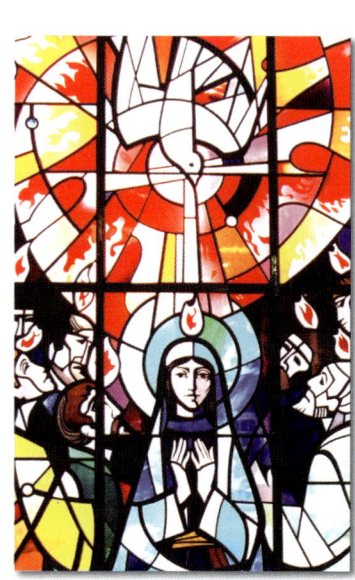

Activities

1. Peter and the apostles knew what Jesus expected of them, but lacked the courage to do it. However, when they received the Holy Spirit, Peter spoke out with conviction and confidence.
   a) Imagine you are Peter being interviewed by a journalist from the Jerusalem Times who has read Acts 2: 22-24 and 2: 37-41.
      Here are the questions:
      - Your sudden courage to speak out seems very out of character for a group of men who were lying low. How do you explain it? Were you drunk?
      - I'm told 3,000 were added to your numbers. You asked them to be baptised. What does that mean?
      - Why did Jesus inspire you?
   b) Write a detailed reply to each question for the journalist.

2. Time and time again, the apostles worked miracles.
   They were stoned, shipwrecked or ended up in prison but God was with them in spectacular ways.
   a) Work in pairs or small groups. Recreate some of the most momentous events in the lives of the apostles.
      Some references to help from the Acts of the Apostles:

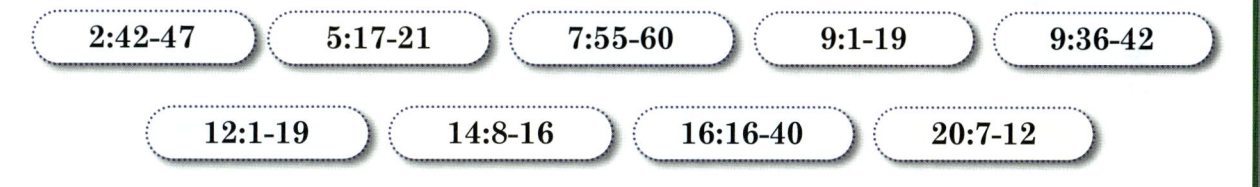

   | 2:42-47 | 5:17-21 | 7:55-60 | 9:1-19 | 9:36-42 |
   | 12:1-19 | 14:8-16 | 16:16-40 | 20:7-12 |

   b) You have two minutes to dramatise your scene.

3. a) What do you think sustained the apostles and enabled them to face the challenges?
   b) How might these events influence our beliefs and values?

4. From your study of the lives of the apostles, what advice might you be able to offer to a person who:
   a) was wrongly accused;
   b) was mocked because of his or her belief in Jesus;
   c) lost his or her job because what was requested was contrary to the teaching of the Church so refused to do it.

*Deepen our understanding of the gifts of the Spirit.
Reflect on how these gifts relate to daily life.*

Gifts of the Spirit

Sometimes we are timid and fearful about professing our faith in public. This is partly because we are not aware of the gifts offered to us in the Sacrament of Confirmation. If we understand the gifts God offers us and truly believe we receive them in this Sacrament, then it is possible for our lives to be transformed. In that way, we can touch the lives of many people.

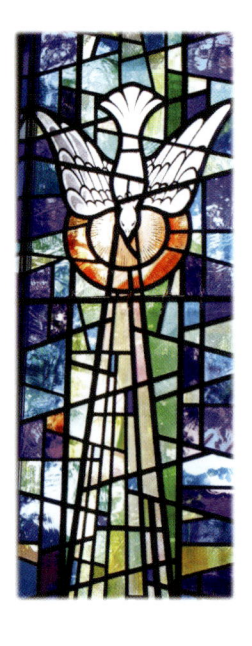

- Wisdom
- Understanding
- Right Judgement
- Courage
- Knowledge
- Reverence
- Awe and Wonder

Gift of Wisdom

Wisdom is the gift to see things as Jesus sees them.
- It is like a divine instinct which helps us to understand that the wisdom of God is far greater than the wisdom of the world.
- It helps us to recognise what is of genuine value.
- It helps us to understand the importance of developing a relationship with God.

Our mother, Mary, possessed this gift. When the angel Gabriel spoke to her, she responded, "Let what God wants be done unto me" (Lk. 1:38).

The opposite is placing all one's trust in earthly values, for example:
- money, wealth, status and power.

Activities

1. How does Mary's 'Yes' to God help us? Explain in detail.[14]

2. a) Read about
   - the man who built his house on sand (Mt. 7:24-27);
   - the man who built barns to store his riches (Lk. 12:16-21).
   b) What is the lesson for us in each of them?
   c) Write a modern day parable to illustrate this gift of wisdom.

[14] See *The Way*, pp. 31 and 36-38

Gift of Understanding

This is a spiritual understanding which helps us grasp the meaning of the death and resurrection of Jesus.

It helps us to understand how we meet Jesus;
- to find him when we are suffering;
- to look ahead with courage in life;
- to discover and appreciate the wonders of creation.

Jesus had this spiritual understanding when he knew he would have to suffer, be rejected by his own people and be put to death. Nevertheless, it was in and through this suffering that Jesus rose again and made it possible for those who believe in him to share eternal life in heaven.

The opposite is:
- not to have the courage to face up to difficulties;
- to lose heart when our secular society scorns religious belief.

Activity

Think about the difficulties young people experience.
Give two examples of how the gift of understanding could help them.

Gift of Right Judgement

It is the ability to choose what is truly good.
- It helps us to choose between two 'goods' which clash with each other, to choose the one that corresponds to the will of God.
- This gift allows us to see what God desires for us.
- It restores peace and helps us to make courageous decisions.

Archbishop Romero had this gift. He could see that "the world that the Church must serve is the world of the poor".

The opposite is:
- to have a misguided conscience and be confused;
- to give in to the opinion of others without thinking through the right course of action.

Activity

Work in pairs. Think of a situation which could leave a young person very confused and anxious. Share how you think the gift of right judgement may help that person.

Gift of Courage
This gift gives moral strength and helps us to profess our faith when faced with dangers.
- It gives us the courage to stand up for what we believe when others don't agree.
- It helps us overcome the fear of death because we will feel we are in the hands of God.

St. Maximilian Kolbe, a prisoner in Auschwitz, had this gift. When a father of a family pleaded to be spared execution, Maximilian spoke up and said, "I am a Catholic priest. I am willing to take his place." As a result, he was condemned to die in the starvation cell. Now he is canonized a saint.

The opposite is:
- to be afraid to admit that we are a Catholic;
- to be afraid of what being a committed Catholic might involve;
- to be cowardly like Peter when he denied knowing Jesus.

Pause to Reflect
Think of possible occasions when you will need this gift. Pray for it.

Gift of Knowledge
The spiritual gift of knowledge helps us to see things from God's point of view.
- It helps us to see and understand the needs of other people.

St. John Vianney possessed this gift. He was a parish priest in a small village in France. He was a humble man and he knew how to explain the mysteries of God to all the people. Thousands of people flocked to him for confession. He knew their deep needs and read their hearts.

The opposite is:
- to see things only in relation to their material value;
- to think science alone has the answer.

Activities
"The eye of the world does not see further than this life … But the eye of the Christian sees into the depths of eternity." St. John Vianney
Give an example to explain what this means.

Gift of Reverence
This gift helps us to pray from our heart.
- It enables us to speak with God and call Him Father or Abba (Dad).
- It urges us to give glory to God in everything we do.

St. Thérèse of Lisieux possessed this gift. When she was extremely ill, she wrote: "My heaven lies in always resting before my God".

The opposite is:
- having no love or respect for God;
- not believing that each one of us is a child of God;
- not understanding other people or being willing to show them love.

Pause to Reflect
Do I make time each day to be alone with God?
Do I spend time with my family?

Gift of Awe and Wonder
It helps us to recognise the presence of God and seek His friendship.
- It is having great reverence for the mystery of God.
- It helps us to see creation as the work of God.
- It helps us to think carefully about the way we treat others.

Mother Teresa of Calcutta possessed this gift because she had a profound reverence towards the presence of God in the poor, the dying and those suffering from diseases.

Jesus warns us about the opposite.
- Woe to you who neglect justice and the love of God.
- Woe to you who load people with burdens hard to bear and you yourselves do not lift a finger to ease them. (Lk. 11:39-46)

Activity
"I don't do great things; I do little things with great love." Mother Teresa of Calcutta
Give examples of how you could do the same.

Pause to Reflect
Gifts of the Spirit – Power Point presentation.

Activities

1. Work in pairs. Decide on your top ten **Key Points to Remember** in the gifts of the Spirit.

2. God is offering you these gifts. Which two would be most helpful to you? Why?

3. Secular humanists, who do not believe in God, frequently wish to identify belief in God as the problem in life.
   Use your knowledge of the gifts of God's Spirit to draft a letter to them to explain that **'God is not the problem in the world but a gift to be discovered'**.
   You will need to reflect on how these gifts can help all of us in our daily lives.

4. Work in groups. Choose one gift of the Holy Spirit. Think of an imaginative way to present this gift to the class. Highlight the transforming power of this gift in a person's life.

5. a) Watch the Power Point presentation on Jane Tomlinson.
   b) Write a blurb that could be used for the cover of a DVD about her. Think about her suffering, courage, faith, determination, selflessness, generosity, etc.
   c) Which gifts of the Holy Spirit are most obvious in her life?

Understand what the Sacrament of Confirmation means. Reflect on the commitment it involves.

The Sacrament of Confirmation

What does the Sacrament of Confirmation do for us?

Let us go back to the time the apostles were in the Upper Room. They didn't understand what Jesus meant when he promised to send his Spirit. Like us, they wondered what this Spirit would do for them, they were fearful and afraid. Then, it all suddenly happened. When the Holy Spirit came upon them they were transformed into courageous witnesses of Jesus.

Confirmation is for us what Pentecost was for the apostles. They were filled with the power from on high and were inspired to be witnesses to all that Jesus had taught them. In addition, they were given the courage to go out and teach about Jesus.

For us, we received the Holy Spirit when we were baptised. The Sacrament of Confirmation strengthens, confirms and perfects what has already been given in Baptism. In addition, the person receiving the Sacrament of Confirmation is commissioned to be an 'official' public witness to Jesus Christ and more strictly obliged to spread and defend the faith by word and deed. We are called to become the public representatives of Jesus, not only to speak for him but to act in his name.

In this Sacrament, we receive the gifts of the Spirit. These gifts strengthen us to share in the public mission of the Church. Jesus has called us personally to share this mission. It is when we place absolute trust in him and start to live out our mission that we will receive the strength to do so. For each one of us it will be different because we are all unique.

Pause to Reflect

In the Sacrament of Confirmation a person is commissioned to be an 'official' public witness to Jesus. This person is more strictly obliged to defend the faith by word and deed.
- In what ways can a person give public witness?
- Think of two things you can start doing this week.

A letter from Cardinal Carlo Maria Martini to a boy preparing for Confirmation:

Confirmation is the moment in which you complete what the teachers of long ago used to call your journey of Christian initiation. The gift of the Spirit makes you a living stone in that dwelling place of God amidst humanity that we call the Church.

The Church counts on you for its existence; even though you are very young, you're able and ready to become, like Jesus, one who serves. You will receive a gift, but it's a heavy gift; I'd call it a seed that can bear wonderful fruit.

Activity

"The Church counts on you for its existence."
   a) Explain what you understand by the Church.[15]
   b) Why does the Cardinal think it counts on YOU for its existence?
   c) Do you agree? Say what you think and why.
   d) Give a different point of view and explain why others hold it.

Where possible, support your views with reference to Scripture or the teaching of the Church.

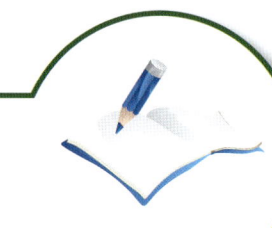

Seeds bearing fruit!

Some young people were invited to write about their experience of receiving the Sacrament of Confirmation. Here are their replies.

Magda

"I made my confirmation because I felt ready and responsible. I wanted a stronger relationship with God. This has affected my life. I feel like a new person so I have started from fresh to help people around me. I can solve my problems differently because I know God is with me."

[15] See *The Truth* pp. 90-93

Emmanuel

"I made my confirmation because I wanted to confirm the choice that my parents had made for me when I was baptised as a baby. I wanted people to know that it was my choice to lead a Christian life and be the sort of person who cared about people rather than money or fame. Some of my friends thought I was crazy. I didn't care, it was my decision. Since I have received the Sacrament of Confirmation, I have not really done things but I have talked to my friends about why I want to live the sort of life Jesus taught us about. It is not just about going to heaven; it is about making this world a better place and I plan to do something about it."

Andy

"It took me a while to decide about being confirmed because I knew I was going to have to take my faith in God seriously; go to Mass every week and live out the commitment. Eventually, I accepted an offer to make a Retreat with others – we had good fun, I got to know some people really well. We thought about *important* stuff and I got in touch with the spiritual part of me – that inner part which I usually neglect. By the end of the Retreat, I knew I wanted to receive the Sacrament of Confirmation.

One way in which I live out my commitment is to visit an elderly man and his wife. He is house-bound and I am teaching him computer skills. He was excited when I showed him how to surf the internet, now he is even able to send emails to his family in Australia. I pop in every week as he usually wants to know more, he even wants Skype."

Angeline

"My reasons for getting confirmed were to fully take on responsibility for my own faith and celebrate God's presence in my life. By accepting the Sacrament of Confirmation, I was acknowledging to my family, friends and to God that I was going to be responsible for living in God's way.

As a result, an important piece of my life is my work with HCPT - the Handicapped Children's Pilgrimage Trust. Through HCPT, we care one-to-one for disabled and disadvantaged children before and during the pilgrimage. As I become more involved, the challenges increase but the friendship of others helps us to get through even the hardest of times. The sense of belonging, not only to the Church but also to a smaller group within the Church, is good and the fact that you are helping people less fortunate than yourself gives a great sense of achievement. The love of God is experienced all around, both in Lourdes and in the preparation for the pilgrimage."

Activities

1. a) Use bullet points to list the main reasons given on pages 60-62 above for receiving the Sacrament of Confirmation.
   b) Add any good reasons you think are missing to the list.

2. When we receive the Sacrament of Confirmation, we are called to witness to our faith, to speak out for justice, to do all we can to defend and promote human rights. Choose one of the following and suggest what young people can do to help those who are:
   - disabled;
   - weak and vulnerable;
   - homeless;
   - refugees;
   - asylum seekers.

*Understand the rite of the Sacrament of Confirmation.
Reflect on the impact of this Sacrament on our lives.*

The Rite of the Sacrament of Confirmation

Blessed Pope John Paul II

When you receive the Sacrament of Confirmation, "Jesus' gift of the Holy Spirit is going to be poured out upon you in a particular way. You will hear the words of the Church spoken over you, calling upon the Holy Spirit to *confirm your faith, to seal you in his love, to strengthen you for his service.* You will then take your place among fellow-Christians throughout the world, full citizens now of the People of God. You will witness to the truth of the Gospel in the name of Jesus Christ. You will live your lives in such a way as to make holy all human life. Together with all the confirmed, you will become living stones in the cathedral of peace. Indeed, you are called by God to be instruments of His peace….

My dear young people, the world of today needs you, for it needs men and women who are filled with the Holy Spirit. It needs your courage and hopefulness, your faith and perseverance. The world of tomorrow will be built by you."

Activities

1. "The world of today needs you …. The world of tomorrow will be built by you."
   What values would you like to promote in this world?
   Use a page to draw large building blocks for a cathedral. On each block write suggestions for bringing peace into:
   - family life;
   - school;
   - local community.

2. Illustrate ways in which the Holy Spirit could help you build the world of tomorrow.

Rite of the Sacrament of Confirmation

The Sacrament of Confirmation is conferred during the celebration of Mass. After the Gospel, the priest presents the candidates to the Bishop. The Bishop invites the candidates to renew their Baptismal Promises by rejecting Satan and accepting the truths of the Catholic faith.

The Prayer of Consecration: the Bishop extends his hands over the whole group of confirmands. Since the time of the apostles this gesture has signified the gift of the Spirit. The Bishop invokes the outpouring of the Spirit in these words:

"My dear friends, in baptism, God our Father gave the new birth of eternal life to His chosen sons and daughters.
Let us pray to our Father that He will pour out the Holy Spirit to strengthen His sons and daughters with His gifts and anoint them to be more like Jesus Christ the Son of God.

All powerful God, Father of our Lord Jesus Christ,
by water and the Holy Spirit
You freed your sons and daughters from sin
and gave them new life.
Send your Holy Spirit upon them
to be their helper and guide.
Give them the spirit of wisdom and understanding,
The spirit of right judgement and courage,
the spirit of knowledge and reverence.
Fill them with the spirit of wonder and awe in your presence.
We ask this through Christ our Lord."

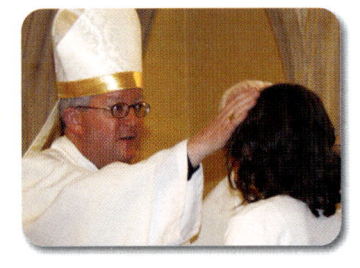

The Sacrament of Confirmation is now conferred through the anointing with chrism on the forehead. This is done by the laying on of the hand, and through the words
"Be sealed with the gift of the Holy Spirit".

Key Points to Remember
Confirmation gives us the same Holy Spirit that the apostles received at Pentecost.
- This sacrament *perfects* what was begun at Baptism.
- It deepens our union with God.
- It strengthens our bond with the Church.
- It commissions us to witness and work for the spread of God's Kingdom.

Activities

1. Before receiving the Sacrament of Confirmation, you need to have been baptised. Why do you think this is necessary?

2. As soon as you receive the Sacrament of Confirmation your friends are going to ask you:
    - what happened?
    - how do you now feel?
    - how is it likely to affect your life?

   Prepare answers and share them with the person next to you.

3. Explain how attendance at Mass will give strength, courage and support to sustain our mission. Think about what happens at:
    - the Penitential Rite;
    - the Liturgy of the Word;
    - the Offertory;
    - the Consecration;
    - Holy Communion;
    - the Final Blessing.

Have some understanding of the meaning of discernment. Reflect on its importance.

Discernment

To discern is to see clearly with our mind and our senses the right course of action. As Christians, if we want to find out what God is asking of us, it is not just a matter of deciding on what appears to be right and wrong. It's about sifting through our inner experiences to see if they truly come from God's Spirit.

Discernment involves:
- identifying what it is we want to discern;
- gathering all the information and facts about the matter to be discerned;
- opening our heart to God in prayer so that He can really be **God** in our life.
- sifting through our inner experiences through the daily exercise outlined on page 66.

Discerning God's Will

Experience
- What do I find rewarding? Why?
- What do I find boring? Why?

Talents
- What am I good at?
- What do I enjoy most of all?
- What can I learn from my mistakes?

Service
- Who do I help? Why?
- How does it make me feel?

Prayer
- Set aside a time each day to be alone with Jesus.
- Reflect on the last twenty-four hours. Think about what has been good or difficult and why.
- Call to mind that Jesus comes into our lives through these experiences.
- Stay quietly with Jesus. If any thoughts come to your mind write them in your diary.

Advice
- What do others say about me?
- What advice do other people give me?
  - Family
  - Friends
  - Teachers

(This activity should be done on a sheet of paper for your own personal benefit only.)
Take some time now to be alone with Jesus. Decide on a time when you could do this daily.
- In prayer, what questions about your future do you want answered?
- Reflect on the last twenty-four hours. What has been good or difficult? Why?
- What experiences do I find rewarding? Why?
- What do I find boring? Why?
- What am I good at?
- What do I enjoy most of all?
- What can I learn from my mistakes?
- Who do I help? Why? How does that make me feel?
- What do my family, friends and teachers say about me?

66

Pope Benedict XVI speaks to young people

On 18 September 2010, Pope Benedict spoke to 2,500 young people who had gathered to greet him outside Westminster Cathedral in London.

The focal point of his message was: "I ask you to look into your hearts, each day, to find the source of all true love. Jesus is always there, quietly waiting for us to be still with him and to hear his voice. Deep within your heart, he is calling you to spend time with him in prayer, but this kind of prayer, real prayer, requires discipline. It requires time for moments of silence every day. Often, it means waiting for the Lord to speak.

Even amidst the busyness and stress of our daily lives, we need to make space for silence, because it is in silence that we find God. And, it is in silence that we discover our true self.

It is in discovering our true self, that we discover the particular vocation which God has given us for the building up of His Church and the redemption of our world. Heart speaks unto heart: with these words from my heart, dear young friends, I assure you of my prayers for you."

Activities

1. a) Write down the key points from Pope Benedict XVI's address to young people.
   b) Think of some way to make sure you will hold on to them.

2. Developing a skill, talent or interest requires discipline.
   a) What do you have to do, or not do, to develop one of your skills, talents or interests?
   b) Compare this with the discipline needed to develop your relationship with Jesus.

*Know about some people whose lives have been transformed by the Spirit.
Think about how their experience can help us.*

Transformed by the Spirit

"You did not choose me,
no, I chose you;
and I commissioned you
to go out and to bear fruit,
fruit that will last …" (Jn. 15:16).

Each one of us is chosen and loved by God. In and through the sacraments we receive the life and love of Jesus. If we remain faithful to him, he will be with us guiding and directing our path. Read the following examples of the transforming power of the Spirit of Jesus.

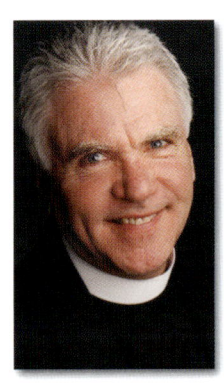

Brother Rick Curry SJ

Born with no forearm, Rick Curry had to face many challenges. While his mother brought him up to be totally independent, he knew from an early age that the world saw him as disabled.

He believed God called him to religious life with the Society of Jesus, the Jesuits. However, he had yet to discover what the gifts were that God had given to him and how to use them.

Rejection

As a young Jesuit Brother, having his master's and doctoral degrees in Theatre, he was sent out to audition for a mouthwash commercial. He never got the chance, for he didn't get past the receptionist who pointed at his missing right forearm and laughed him out of the room.

Rick was filled with anger, hurt and shame. Gradually, through prayer, he understood that by being angry and ashamed of his disability, he was rejecting a gift from God. He had to learn that everything that comes to us is a gift from God. Our challenge is to discern how to use those gifts. Later, he understood that a person grows in direct proportion to how much they have accepted their disability.

Acceptance and Transformation

Two months later, Rick decided to start a non-profit theatre programme where all disabled people would be welcome. In 1977, the National Theatre Workshop of the Handicapped (NTWH) was opened in New York.

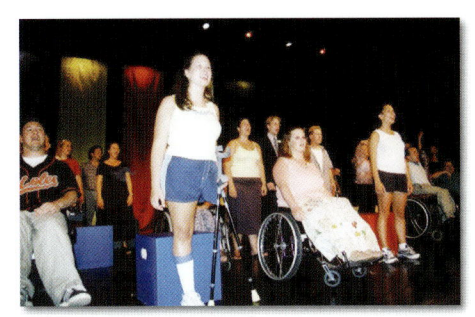

Some NTWH participants, like Rick, were born with their disabilities; others had their bodies broken in sudden and terrible ways. "You can start to feel like you're the only person you know who's dealing with … whatever," he said. "It's empowering to be around others with a disability. We believe in the celebration of our differences."

Brother Rick Curry has now trained more than 15,000 disabled artists.

Activities

"There is an amazing grace that comes when you embrace your difference, your brokenness and go on from there." Rick Curry SJ

Some young people suffer from various types of brokenness:
- poor self-image;
- depression;
- addiction;
- physical or mental impairment.

What steps can we take to support one another? Discuss.

Life in its Fullness

After forty-six years of being called Brother, Rick Curry SJ was ordained a priest in September 2009. How did it happen?

It was through a meeting with a disabled veteran that God was to speak to Rick. The veteran was a triple amputee using his prosthetic legs for the first time. He arrived, soaking wet, in appalling weather conditions. Rick says they talked for a long time. "He had so much bottled-up anger but he felt comfortable with me, because like him, I have only one forearm. He told me about his experiences and asked for absolution. When I said I couldn't absolve him, he became more furious. I explained that I was a brother and had never been called to be a priest".

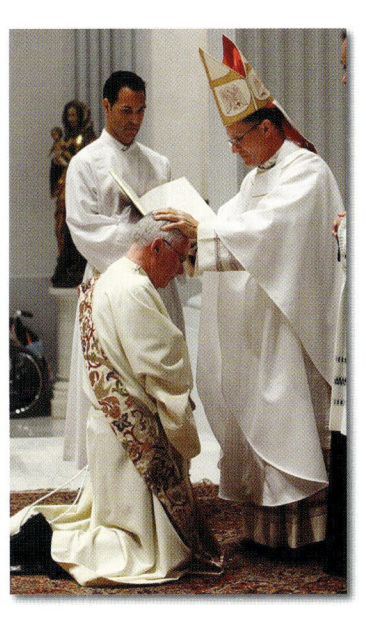

It was when Rick was approached by other veterans asking him to hear their confession, that he knew this call was from God.

Disabled veterans, men and women, of the wars in Iraq and Afghanistan became part of Rick's life.

Rick had never thought about the priesthood, he'd been happy as a brother. Besides he was sixty years old. Veterans needing a priest convinced him. "They kept coming," he said. "They needed sacramental ministry that I couldn't give them." Rick took time out to study for the priesthood and is now ordained.

Fr. Rick is now developing the Academy for Veterans, a one-year transitional programme that will enable them to go to Georgetown University. "These wounded warriors and their families have sacrificed so much," he said. "They have been blinded, lost limbs, and some are even paralyzed. And no matter what you may think of wars, these soldiers are serving us, yet their lives are in tatters when they come home. We cannot let these heroes be marginalised and forgotten!" Fr. Rick is able to help them recognise what God is asking of them. He has opened the 'Wounded Warriors' workshop and expects that this will bring about much healing and growth.

Activities

1. Identify and explain how the gifts of the Spirit have been present in Fr. Rick's life.

2. a) If Fr. Rick was going to write his autobiography, what do you think he would call it? Why?
   b) Write the back cover for this autobiography to encourage others to read it.
   c) Share the story with others and invite them to contribute comments to the back cover.

3. In what ways do you think the 'Wounded Warriors' workshop will bring about healing and growth?

Missionary in a Wheelchair: Aldo Giachi SJ (1927-1989)

Aldo Giachi was born in Stia, Italy, on 11 April 1927. When he was six years old, his mother died tragically and a little later, his father. Then when he was seventeen, he entered the Jesuit novitiate. However, he had to leave one year later to have a painful operation for a gastric ulcer.

A few years later, he returned to the novitiate and made his first vows in April 1948. Aldo moved to Rome to complete his studies for the priesthood at the Gregorian University. In 1950, when he was twenty-three years old, he was laid low with a spinal tumour which paralysed his limbs and put him in a wheelchair for life. The doctors said surgery was too risky and gave him one year to live.

Thanks to his extraordinary determination, he completed his theology studies and received permission from Pope Pius XII to be ordained a priest. Not long after, to the astonishment of everyone, Aldo asked to be sent as a missionary to Chile, South America.

> Role-play the conversation you think Aldo would have had with his superior when he requested to go to South America.

Fr. Aldo Giachi in South America

Following a process of discernment, on 12 April 1968, Aldo left from Rome airport with two nurses who would remain with him as there was little he could do for himself.

Fr. Aldo wanted to transform his daily handicap and suffering into an extraordinary apostolate of service to people limited physically, like himself. He firmly believed in the words of Jesus: **"I have come that you may have life and have it to the full".**

He was appointed chaplain at the El Salvador Hospital in Santiago where there were 1,800 beds. Every afternoon and sometimes at night, he would visit the patients and on occasions, give them the Sacrament of the Sick. In the mornings, he spent hours visiting the sick in their homes. Also, he gave talks to the hospital nurses and chaplains.

Fr. Aldo Giachi extends his horizons

Fr. Aldo was dreaming of an apostolate on a much larger scale. While he was totally dependent on others, he placed absolute trust in God and threw himself headlong into a series of initiatives. Through appeals on television and radio, he invited others to help him.

Instead of his physical handicap being an obstacle, he shared how it led him to value suffering and place himself in the hands of God. He invited the disabled not to close in on themselves but to become aware of the value in God's eyes of suffering accepted out of love.

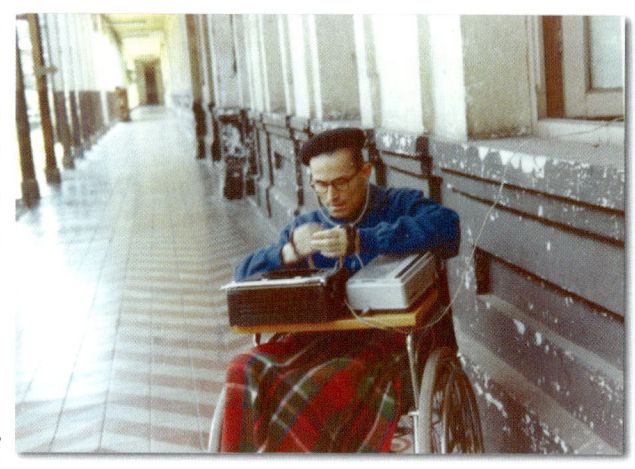

In 1970, Fr. Aldo had a large centre built for chronically ill people, those who would never get better. He appealed to young people to work on Saturdays and Sundays to help build it. They were eager to do so.
This centre was also used for him to give retreats to people who were ill.

He raised funds to buy wheelchairs for the housebound and then made it possible for many sick people who had never taken a trip or even crossed the city in a car, to go on outings in cars and buses.

Fr. Aldo was helped by generous volunteers because he was able to share with them his ideal of living for the poor of God. The Jesuits gave him the use of a large house with thirty bedrooms. This became a holiday home for the handicapped people. Then, Fr. Aldo found other centres in different parts of the country for them as well.

In 1978, he went to Brazil. Here he made contacts to start up centres like those in Chile. He received gifts of two buildings from the Bishop of Sào Paolo. He distributed 10,000 copies of a publicity brochure for his work. On returning to Chile, he was invited to several dioceses to inspire others to start similar projects.

On 20 July 1989, Aldo was admitted to hospital. He was seriously ill. He was unable to speak but his eyes expressed the offering of his own suffering to Jesus. Twenty-fours hours later, in great peace, he passed away.

The next morning, his body was taken to 'Our Hope' centre for a wake with the disabled and with friends, while the grey skies promised long-awaited rain.

Fr. Aldo's funeral was a celebration of his life. The Cardinal of Santiago was present with fifty Jesuits. A huge circle of people in wheelchairs surrounded the coffin. During the Mass a large rainbow appeared in the sky – this was taken as the first sign from heaven sent by Fr. Aldo Giachi SJ.

Activities

1. Evaluate the life and ministry of Fr. Aldo Giachi SJ. Think about:
   - what he must have suffered;
   - the choices open to him;
   - the path he chose to follow;
   - how he spent his time;
   - the effect it had on others: volunteers and handicapped;
   - how he can help us today.

2. An extract from Fr. Aldo's diary: "In working with the sick it's hugely important to smile, to be near them, listen to them, comfort them, console them, tell them stories and cheer them up, in the hope of giving them something more at the right moment."
   a) What does it tell you about Fr. Aldo's character?
   b) What do you think he meant by 'giving them something more at the right moment'? Explain and give an example.

3. Imagine Fr. Aldo had the opportunity to use television and radio today. Write or record the use you think he would make of this opportunity to **'help the poor of God'**.

4. "God's power is greatest when we are aware of our own weakness and completely trust in Him."
   Discuss this statement with reference to the life of Fr Aldo Giachi SJ.

4. God's Call

Know that God calls each person who seeks to do His will. Reflect on the different ways God calls.

God calls each person

"There is a variety of gifts but always the same Spirit; there are all sorts of services to be done, but always to the same Lord; working in all sorts of different ways in different people, it is the same God who is working in all of them." (1Cor. 12:4-6)

I wonder what is God asking of me?

From the beginning of our time at school, we are encouraged to think about our future – what do we want to be? Often the answer to this question is to say that we want to be a doctor, a mechanic, a journalist or some other job. Or we might say that we want to be rich, successful or even famous.

A different way of answering the question is to think about what sort of person we want to be, or what sort of person God wants us to be. All of us want to be generous, loving and courageous. Most of all, we want to do what is right in fulfilling God's plan for us.

Activities

1. Copy and complete the grid below. For the column on the left, think about achievements, for example, a job or profession. On the right, think about your character and how you would like to be described by others.

What do I want to achieve?	What do I want to be?

2. a) What types of gifts are valued in society today? Why?
   b) Which of these gifts make a difference to people's lives? How?

Let Go, Let God

Sometimes, the constant and relentless need to be in touch with others and the media can block out time to be in touch with ourselves. There is a tendency to switch from laptop to iPad to iPhone and then to the TV as days pass into nights. Perhaps this need for electronic gadgets has dulled our awareness of the need for inner peace and stillness. If these needs are ignored, we may only live at the level of computerised robots.

The good news is that it is not all or nothing. It is a matter of making sure there is a **balance** in our lives, a balance which makes time for the God of our lives so that we know who God is and what He wants of us. God comes to us every day in people, events and circumstances. We need to be ready with an open heart to welcome Him into our lives.

To let go, let God, means we have to **give God a real place** in our daily lives; to have a relationship with Him and to seek to do His will.

> "God has created me to do Him some definite service; He has committed some work to me which He has not committed to another. I have my mission - I may never know it in this life, but I shall be told it in the next. I am a link in a chain, a bond of connection between persons. He has not created me for naught. I shall do good, I shall do His work; I shall be an angel of peace, a preacher of truth in my own place, while not intending it, if I do but keep His commandments and serve Him in my calling."
>
> Blessed John Henry Newman

Activities

1. Use the grid on average earnings in this country. (WS TB & DVD ROM)
   a) List the jobs in order of importance.
   b) What important gifts do people at the top of your list have?

2. With reference to Mt. 6:19-24, design a webpage showing how we should live if we are to gain entry into the Kingdom of God.

3. What does 'Let God, Let God' mean for you? (WS DVD ROM)

Know that some people are called to a specific mission. Reflect on the various ways God uses them to help others.

God's call to a specific mission

When will you answer my call? GOD

When did God call me?

What does God want with me?

How will I answer God's call?

God's call not only comes in a variety of ways, but to people in various walks of life: "All the faithful of Christ of whatever rank or status, are called to the fullness of the Christian life and to the perfection of charity. They must follow in His footsteps and conform themselves to His image, seeking the will of the Father in all things. They must devote themselves with all their being to the glory of God and the service of their neighbour."[16]

This means that everybody who truly seeks the Lord has a mission or a vocation. For some, it is as lay-people who for various reasons are single, for others it may be a vocation to marriage, religious life or priesthood.

God's unexpected call

In 1982, as a student, Peter Walters bought a very cheap flight to Colombia for a holiday.

He enjoyed his holiday. But when he went to book his return flight trouble began. His open ticket meant he had to wait two whole weeks to get back to Great Britain.

[16] *Lumen Gentium*, 40

His money had almost run out, so he had to decide whether to sleep in the street and be able to buy a snack or stay in a cheap hotel room and go hungry. Knowing the streets were dangerous, he chose the latter.

Outside Peter's hotel was a group of dirty, scruffy, cheeky young lads and as he left the hotel each day they tried to beg from him. They found it hard to believe he was a foreigner without money. To convince them, he told them what happened. They offered to take him under their wing, shared their food and generally kept him safe on the street. In short, they 'adopted' him.

Naturally, Peter wanted to hear their story. Why were they in the street, so dirty and neglected? Why were they not at home or at school? What they said appalled him. Families had been displaced by the violence of Colombia's long-running civil war and drugs wars. They were forced to leave their rural homes for the violent shanty-towns of the cities. Some of their parents were killed and their step-parents often subjected the children to physical and sexual abuse. Children were sent out to work. If they went home with little or no money, they would be beaten and so they chose not to return. Worst of all, there were those who regarded these children as rubbish and called them 'The Disposable Ones'. At times, they did indeed dispose of them.

Moved by the children's compassion for him, Peter was unable to forget all he had heard. He felt compelled to go to see the Archbishop. The Archbishop listened to him carefully. He agreed that the situation for Colombia's street-children was indeed desperate and that the Church was trying to do something to help them but that the problem was enormous. "Have you considered," he said, "that God may be asking you to do something about it?"

Some days later, Peter left Colombia, but he could not forget the children or the Archbishop's words. He spent time discerning what God was really asking of him.

It was ten years later when Peter was finally in a position to return to Colombia to help street-children. He is now ordained and has established a Charitable Trust known as 'Let the Children Live'. He has recruited a team of helpers. Their mission is to save and transform the lives of as many street-children as possible and to prevent others from having to take to the streets.

Activities

1. Imagine you are Peter Walters. Write three postcards to friends at home:
   - the first after four days in the cheap hotel room;
   - the second after meeting the children;
   - the third after meeting the Archbishop.

2. 'God or coincidence'?
   Things happen for a reason. Often the reason is not clear at the time.
   But later, we discover what God's plan was.
   a) Trace God's plan for Peter Walters in the circumstances of his life.
   b) How might his experience help us when we meet with difficulties and our plans go wrong?

3. God's mysterious ways in the life of Mary Butterwick (WS TB & DVD ROM)
   a) What choices did Mary Butterwick have?
   b) Mary went from **'freedom from'** her own will to **'freedom for'** God to lead her. What did she do to enable this to happen?

4. Identify three steps on Mary Butterwick's path to transformation.

5. Imagine you are a background researcher. You are sent to interview Mary Butterwick about her work prior to a TV appearance.
   a) Read the information about her (WS TB & DVD ROM). What questions would you ask her?
   b) Write down her replies.
   c) Produce a report for the interviewer which gets to the heart of Mary Butterwick's life and source of inspiration.

6. Imagine your local radio has invited you to give a 'Thought for the Day' on 'Trusting in God'. Write it out. You may wish to think of:
   - your own experience;
   - the experience of someone you know;
   - the experience of Peter Walters or Mary Butterwick.

Understand the vocation to Marriage.
Think about the reasons why people get married.

What is a Vocation?

A vocation means a 'call' to a particular way of life in the service of God. Your vocation is what God calls you to do with your life. Everyone is called by God to know, love and serve Him in this life. This is the key to eternal happiness.

We are called to be happy – true happiness comes from living out our vocation. It is finding our purpose in life and living it out. This is what we are all called to do in a variety of different ways.

Having already touched on various types of vocations in this book, our aim now is to focus in particular on the vocation to Marriage, Holy Orders and Religious Life. First, let us pause to reflect on our unique gift.

Who am I?

I am a person …
*special and unique
the only one like me
who can reflect God in my being.*

I am a person …
*a sign of God to others
because I am made in God's image
because I have God's light in my heart
I can mirror God to others.*

I show God to others when I am really me.
*This is what it means to be a person.
This is what it means to be me.*

Activities

Share with the person next to you.
- What are your dreams and hopes for the future?
- What would you be looking for in a relationship?
- Do you believe it is possible to have a life-long relationship?
- What do you think a life-long relationship would involve?

Marriage – what does it involve?

"Marriage is the deepest sharing you can have with another person."

"Marriage thrives on self-giving, love and fidelity."

"The commitment in marriage gives people the opportunity to grow and thrive in ways that other relationships do not."

Marriage is not so much a contract as a **covenant**. A covenant is a very deep and solemn bond of love and trust. It is a pledge to be faithful to one another forever: in good times and in bad times, in sickness and in health, for better or for worse.

Through marriage, a husband and wife give themselves unconditionally to each other. They promise to love each other faithfully for the rest of their lives. They share their joys and sufferings in whatever circumstances life brings them. They express their love through their sexual union which brings them together in the closest intimacy and opens them to the gift of new life.

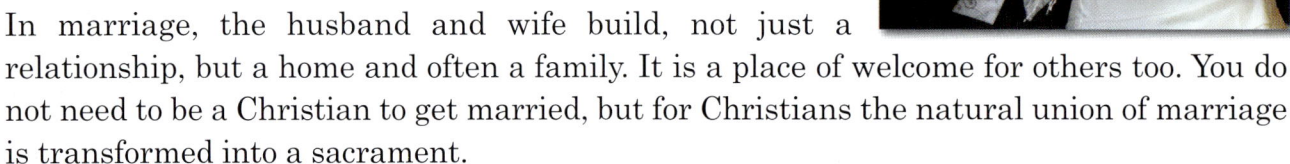

In marriage, the husband and wife build, not just a relationship, but a home and often a family. It is a place of welcome for others too. You do not need to be a Christian to get married, but for Christians the natural union of marriage is transformed into a sacrament.

In and through the Sacrament of Marriage, "Jesus Christ dwells with the husband and wife. He gives them the strength to take up their crosses and to follow him. He gives them the grace to rise again after they have fallen, to forgive one another and to bear one another's burdens."[17]

[17] *Catechism of the Catholic Church*, para. 1642

In this way, the couple love each other with a supernatural love. This supernatural love helps them to forgive human failings. However, it does need the grace of God to sustain it and this comes through daily prayer. It is in this way the marriage becomes a sacrament, for every minute of every day. Every effort to love, serve and be faithful to one another brings God's blessing.

Pause to reflect: The Beauty of Love

The question is asked: "Is there anything more beautiful in life than a young couple with pure hearts clasping hands in the path of marriage? Can there be anything more beautiful than young love?"

And the answer is given. "Yes, there is a more beautiful thing. It is the spectacle of an old man and an old woman finishing their journey together on that path.

Their hands are gnarled, but still clasped; their faces are seamed, but still radiant; their hearts are physically bowed and tired, but still strong with love and devotion for one another. Yes, there is a more beautiful thing than young love. **Old love**." Author Unknown

Activities

1. Marriage is 'love-giving' and 'forgiving'; it is 'life-giving' and 'life-nourishing'. Discuss.
    - Say what you **think** and **why**.
    - Give a different point of view and say why some people hold it.
    - Say why you **disagree** with it.
    - Quote some source of evidence from your study.

2. Reasons for getting married. (WS TB & DVD ROM)

3. Olivia and John are in love. She would like to get married but John would prefer just to live together (to co-habit).
   Write down what you think are:
   a) Olivia's reasons;
   b) John's reasons.
   c) They ask for your opinion. What would you suggest and why?

*Know about the Sacrament of Marriage.
Reflect on its importance.*

The Sacrament of Marriage

It is a **Sacrament** in which God joins man and woman so intimately that "the two become one" (Mk. 10:8).

It is a **Life-Long** commitment for better or for worse, for richer for poorer, in sickness and in health, to love and to cherish, till death separate.

It is a **Covenant** built on a commitment to love and serve one another and to be faithful forever.

It is a **Life-Giving** commitment open to the possibility of having children and bringing them up in the Catholic faith.

Marriage is a solemn covenant between a man and a woman who love each other.

"The love of man and woman is made holy in the Sacrament of Marriage, and becomes the mirror of your everlasting love." (Preface of the Wedding Mass)

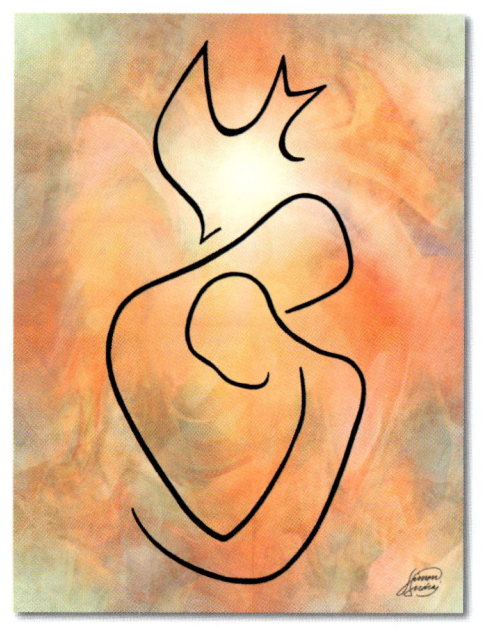

The Sacrament of Marriage is usually celebrated during Mass after the reading of the Gospel and the homily. This is called the Nuptial Mass.

However, it is possible to omit Mass if a Catholic marries someone who does not share his or her faith. A marriage ceremony outside of Mass involves a Liturgy of the Word; the Epistle and Gospel from the Nuptial Mass are read and a blessing is given to the newly married couple.

Conditions Necessary

Usually, the man and woman should have received the Sacrament of Baptism. They must be free to express their consent. They must not be under any pressure or prevented from doing so by any natural or ecclesiastical law.

Rite of the Sacrament of Marriage

Welcome

The ceremony begins when the priest welcomes the couple, their family and friends and assures them that Jesus abundantly blesses their love. They have already been consecrated in the Sacrament of Baptism and now they will be enriched and strengthened by the Sacrament of Marriage.

Statement of Intention

The priest asks the bride and bridegroom if they:

- have come freely and without reservation to give themselves to each other in marriage;
- will love each other as man and wife for the rest of their lives;
- will accept children lovingly from God and bring them up according to the Law of Christ and his Church.

Making Vows

The priest invites the bride and bridegroom to join their right hands and declare their consent before God and His Church.
In turn they say:
"I ……. take you …… ….to be my lawful wedded wife/husband, to have and to hold from this day forward, for better or for worse, for richer or for poorer, in sickness and in health, to love and to cherish, till death do us part".

Blessing and Exchange of Rings

The priest blesses the rings as a sign of love and fidelity and prays that those who wear them may always have a deep faith in each other. The rings are circles which are symbols of eternity. This reminds the couple of God's eternal love for them and of their love for each other.

The husband then places his wife's ring on her finger and she does the same for him saying at the same time, "In the name of the Father and of the Son and of the Holy Spirit. Amen".

Nuptial Blessing

This is a special blessing for the married couple to ask God to enable them to rejoice together in His gift of married love and that they may:
- praise Him when they are happy,
- turn to Him in their sorrows,
- pray to Him in the community of the Church,
- be His witnesses in the world.

The signing of the Marriage Register

This part of the marriage is a legal requirement.

Activities

1. Which five serious conversations do you think a couple should have before deciding to get married?

2. Joe and Sabrina are preparing for their wedding.
    a) What might they want to include in their list of preparations?
    b) What preparations should they make for married life together?
    c) Which set of preparations are the most important? Why?

3. Why do couples get married in front of other people and God? Why do they make their commitment so publicly?

4. Carefully study what takes place in the Sacrament of Marriage. Identify the benefits for the:
    - wife;
    - husband;
    - children;
    - society.

5. Choose one of the following statements:
   "The blessings of a marriage far outweigh the challenges."
   or
   "Marriage is the building block and stability of society."
    - Say what you **think** about this statement and **why**.
    - Give a different point of view and say why some people hold it.
    - Say why you disagree with it.
    - Quote some source of evidence from your study.

6. Plan to interview a couple who have been married for a long time.
    a) Write five questions to ask. Two must be linked to how their faith in God helped them.
    b) After the interview, write your report.

Know about the vocation of a priest.
Think about what the priest does for us.

Priesthood

The life of a priest is an enormous privilege and a great adventure. St. John Vianney, Curé of Ars, France, deeply understood the vocation of a priest:

"O, how great is the priest! ... if he realised what he is, he would die ... God obeys him: he utters a few words and the Lord descends from heaven at his voice, to be contained within a small host". Explaining to his parishioners the importance of the Sacraments, he would say: **"Without the Sacrament of Holy Orders, we would not have the Lord. Who put him there in that tabernacle? The priest. Who feeds your soul and gives it strength for its journey? The priest."**

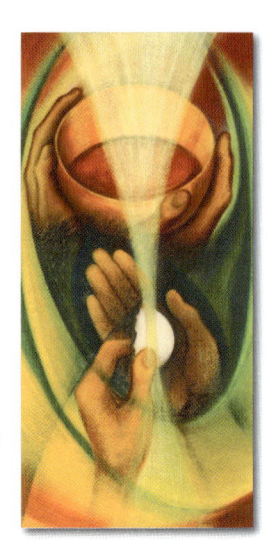

The role and task of the 'ordained priest' is to lead, inspire and guide others. He does this through:
- handing himself over in love to God;
- celebrating the Eucharist;
- living out and teaching the Word of God;
- and with God's help, serving the needs of people.

In this way, the priest acts in the person of Jesus, Head and Shepherd of his Flock.

Activities

1. a) Read 'The Good Shepherd' (Jn. 10:1-15).
      Jesus told this parable to explain his personal care for each one of us.
   b) What do you think are the best ways a priest as 'shepherd of his flock' could support young people?

2. **"The Eucharist makes us Church. The Church cannot be Church, cannot live, exist or survive without the Eucharist."**
   Discuss these statements in relation to the role of the priest.
   Think about:
   - the words of St. John Vianney;
   - the Consecration at Mass;
   - how the Eucharist can help us in everyday life.

The Parish Priest of Ars

St. John Vianney, the Curé of Ars, was proclaimed patron of parish priests worldwide. He was a humble person who had a profound sense of the grace bestowed on the priesthood and what it involved:

He taught his parishioners by example. They knew that if Fr. John Vianney was not kneeling before the tabernacle in the presence of the Blessed Sacrament, he was in the confessional or out visiting the sick and housebound.

As his reputation for helping people in confession spread, the little village of Ars in France became congested with thousands coming to see him. He was very conscious of the devastating effect serious sin has on a person's soul, so much so, that he said: "If we had the faith to see a soul in mortal sin,[18] we would die of fright".

When not visiting the sick and housebound, he would be in the confessional for fifteen hours a day. When asked about this he said: "It is not the sinner who returns to God to beg his forgiveness, but God Himself who runs after the sinner and makes him return to Him". "This good Saviour is so filled with love that He seeks us everywhere". "I impose only a small penance on those who confess their sins properly; the rest of the penance I perform in their place."

St. John Vianney knew that priests are human and might give way to being casual or indifferent about their duties. For this reason, he frequently made vigils and fasts for the good of souls in his care.

Sometimes wealthy people came to him for spiritual direction and would give him money. John Vianney knew this was not for him but for the Church. His secret was, "give everything away; hold nothing back". When he had no money and a poor person knocked at his door, he would say: "Today I'm poor just like you, I'm one of you".

John Vianney taught the crowds to pray by being very faithful to prayer himself. When asked how to pray, he said: "You do not need many words when you pray. I believe in faith that the good and gracious God is there in the tabernacle. We open our souls to Him and feel happy that He allows us to come before Him. This is the best way to pray."

[18] *The Way*, p.98

In a profound way, John Vianney was the shepherd who looked after the flock entrusted to his care. He knew his sheep. He protected them from danger by pointing out to them where they were going wrong and encouraged them to stay close to Jesus in daily prayer.

Activities

1. Why do you think the Church proclaimed St. John Vianney patron of parish priests? Think of three good reasons.

2. Imagine you have the chance to have a conversation with St. John Vianney:
   a) What questions might he ask you?
   b) What answers would you give?

3. The priest acts in the person of Jesus. Explain how he does this. Think about:
   - each of the sacraments;
   - other ways the priest helps people.

Know about the Sacrament of Holy Orders. Think about the blessings and challenges of a priestly vocation.

Sacrament of Holy Orders

The Sacrament of Holy Orders gives a special grace of the Holy Spirit.

Jesus Christ is the Head and Shepherd of the Church. When a man is ordained a priest, the Holy Spirit shapes and moulds him interiorly so that he can represent Jesus. The Holy Spirit gives a special 'SEAL' which is an indelible mark on the soul. This 'seal' cannot be cancelled or wiped away. It has a **spiritual character** and is given **once and forever** – it can never be repeated.

What does the Sacrament actually do to the person?

When the priest receives this **seal**, he represents Jesus as a shepherd who looks after his flock.

Once a man is ordained a priest, he can never stop being a priest, although there might be reasons why he may have to stop doing what a priest does, for example, celebrating the sacraments. The reason for this is that the 'seal' or 'character' impressed within his being, by the special grace of the Holy Spirit, remains forever.

Activities

1. How would you explain to a person of another faith what is meant by the indelible 'seal'? You may use images to help.

2. The grace given in the Sacrament of Holy Orders shapes and moulds the man interiorly.
   What do you understand by this?
   [It may help to use examples from St. John Vianney]

Rite of the Sacrament of Holy Orders

On the day of Ordination, the ceremony is full of outward signs to signify the new life of the priest. The ceremony begins by the Rector of the seminary presenting the candidate for Ordination. He publicly testifies to the Bishop and the people of God that the candidate is ready for Ordination.

The Litany of the Saints

While the candidate lies prostrate on the floor as a sign of abandonment to God, those present call upon the saints to help him. The candidate is aware that this is a total handing-over of himself to the Lord to be available for whatever life demands of him.

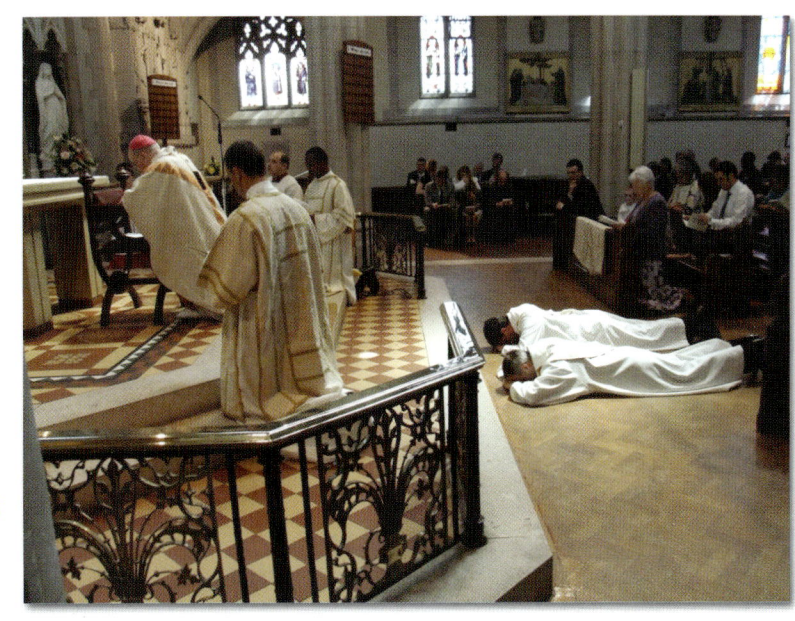

Laying on of Hands

The candidate kneels in front of the Bishop who solemnly imposes his hands on the head of the candidate. This is a gesture of invocation (calling down) of the Holy Spirit and the Bishop says the Prayer of Consecration. At this moment the sacrament takes effect.

Vesting

The new priest receives the stole, the sign of priestly office, which is worn across his shoulders. Then he is given the chasuble, a vestment that covers him entirely. It is the vestment he wears at Mass as a symbol of his service to God and His People.

Anointing

The new priest kneels before the Bishop as he anoints the palms of his hands with the oil of chrism. This is an outward sign of the inner sealing of the priest's heart which is totally dedicated to God.

Celebration of the Eucharist

The new priest receives the bread and wine to be offered in the Mass that he will now celebrate with the Bishop.

Quick Quiz
Write down the meaning of the following words:
- stole
- chasuble
- oil of chrism
- litany of the saints

(Answers on pp.89-90)

Know about the vocation to Religious Life. Reflect on the blessings and challenges of this vocation.

Vocation to Religious Life

A vocation to Religious Life is a call from God to dedicate one's life to living in community. By taking vows of poverty, chastity and obedience, the Religious voluntarily undertakes a life of total dedication to God. This life-style is modelled on the life of the first Christians who shared everything in common. The daily celebration of the Eucharist is at the heart of their lives because it is through living out the Eucharist that they will receive the grace, courage and vision to be joyful witnesses of the Kingdom of God on earth.

The Vows

Poverty – Religious share all things in common. They freely give up the right to own property, believing that God is their only treasure and He alone can satisfy the human heart.

Chastity – Religious give up the possibility of marriage to enter into a unique companionship with Jesus. They strive to love him with an undivided heart and serve him in all people, especially the most needy.

Obedience – This vow involves careful discernment of God's will which at times, may be expressed through the lawful superior and the Holy Rule.

Apostolic and Monastic Religious Life

While there are many forms of Religious life they can generally be classified as either **apostolic** or **monastic**.

Apostolic Religious life focuses on ministry to the Church and to the world. All are committed to spreading the Gospel in a variety of ways depending on their mission or charism.

Monastic life has its focus on contemplative prayer. Its mission is prayer for the Church and the world. The nuns and monks work in the convent or monastery in order to be self-supporting.

Call to Apostolic Religious Life

Sr. Alicia is from Spain and joined the Sisters of the Faithful Companions of Jesus in the USA. She made her final profession in 2006 in Salta, NW of Argentina and is now living in a very poor area. She teaches computer science at the Catholic University. She shares her experience of God's call:

"When I was studying for a PhD in computer science, the idea of a religious vocation swept into my mind. It was exciting, crazy, frightening, incredible, all at the same time. Honestly, I couldn't make much sense of it: here I was, half way through a PhD and thinking of becoming a nun! I had never heard of such a thing. And what a waste of my effort! Plus, I am a very independent person. Surely I could never make a vow of obedience and live in a community of sisters. Yes, I was giving myself all kinds of reasons why this was non-sense. Yet deep inside, I had a strange, almost silly, sense of joy and meaning. I was becoming aware that God was inviting me to deeper intimacy and to become part of Jesus' mission of proclaiming God's love to the world."

In discerning her vocation, Alicia thought deeply about the choice she would be making. She believed it would involve putting aside her work and friends, to be willing to go where her help was most needed in serving others.

"The invitation was so deep and so powerful that I sensed the need to respond to it, placing my life in God's hands. It was an invitation to share in the life and the mission of Jesus, making him present in the world by living as he lived, chaste, poor and obedient. With my commitment, I wanted to be an instrument of the power of Jesus to bring healing, salvation and hope to our world. This conviction and a sense of gratitude for it, is what sustains me day after day."

One of Sr. Alicia's friends who was present when she made her Final Profession later wrote to her:

Dear Sr. Alicia

During the rite of your profession something marvellous happened: A woman – who we in the university know as sane and with a lively intelligence – renounced in front of God Himself:
- *to be a mother,*
- *to have earthly possessions,*
- *her own freedom of choice by pure obedience.*

Also, she committed herself to integrate her 'I' into a communal 'we' and, to complete the circle, to live among those who are marginalized.

This, to the world, is radical foolishness, the complete contradiction of what is proclaimed to the four winds.

But the effect got multiplied when that same woman publicly affirmed, that this was the happiest day of her life. Happiness and renunciation, two sides of the same coin; and, evidently, because of her radiant face, it was completely true.

Activity

a) If you had met Alicia before she made her final decision to enter the convent, what would you have said to her?
b) What questions would you like to ask her now?

Monastic Religious Life

Why become a Poor Clare?
A person has a desire to enter into a mystery which is greater than themselves. This call is somehow always inexplicable; there is an element of the unknown, but God is leading her to a personal relationship with Him.

Formation – being called
The essence of the life of a Poor Clare, is above all else, love – love of Jesus Christ in response to his love. We are all called by God but some people are called to the consecrated life. That means that they give their life to God through living by the vows of poverty, chastity and obedience. They live a simple and uncluttered life under the authority of a superior – the Abbess – whilst giving their heart to God.

Being a Poor Clare
Becoming a nun can take between six to nine years training. A sister in the community accompanies a new candidate known as a postulant. A postulant lives with the community for a year to experience the life and to discover if God is calling her to this way of life. Then the Novitiate lasts for two years. It begins with the postulant receiving the religious habit, learning about the vows and making a commitment to live the monastic way of life. Then, if the community believes that the novice is suited to this way of life, she makes temporary profession for three years. At the end of this time, she can either make final profession or renew her vows for another three years.

A typical day in the life of a Poor Clare
The call to be with God through silence, prayer and manual work is a life lived not for oneself only but for others. The community is called together to be a sign of the kingdom of God, present in the world.

The day begins at 5.00 am and alternates between prayer together in the chapel (the Divine Office and Mass), meditation, spiritual reading, work, meals and recreation. Saint Clare was the first woman in the history of the Church to write her own rule. This form of life enables a balance between an intimacy with God and the joy and challenge of living as sisters in community. Through this experience, the Poor Clare Sisters are challenged to grow in their human relationships and in their relationship with God.

Activities

1. Some people say that Religious Life is an escape from 'real life'; others say it is an impossibly difficult way of life.
   a) In your opinion, what are the advantages and disadvantages of Religious Life?
   b) Imagine your friend tells you that he/she is planning to enter a Religious Order. Think deeply about what you would say to him or her and write it down.

2. Local people in Sutton, Lancashire, call the Church of St. Anne and Blessed Dominic the 'Shrine of the Three Saints': Dominic Barberi, Ignatius Spencer and Elizabeth Prout.
   a) Read about them. (Worksheets on DVD ROM).
   b) Choose one. Identify the main events that enabled this person to offer his or her life totally to God and with God's help to others.
   c) Write a letter to the Vatican in support of this person's canonization.

Blessed Dominic Barberi CP
Born in Italy

Fr, Ignatius Spencer CP
Son of Earl Spencer of Althorp (relation of Princes William and Harry)

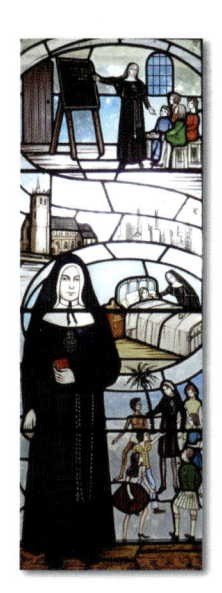

Elizabeth Prout
Born in Shrewsbury

5. Morality & Conscience

Understand the meaning of morality.
Reflect on your own understanding of it.

Morality

What does it mean to be a 'good' person? How would you recognise good behaviour in others or in yourself? Defining the word 'good' is not as straightforward as it may seem. We expect certain standards of behaviour from others and disapprove if they don't measure up.

What do you think 'being good' is?

1. It's producing a good outcome for others.

2. It's being successful.

3. It's doing what's right for me.

4. It's about following the rules.

5. It's going to church and praying regularly.

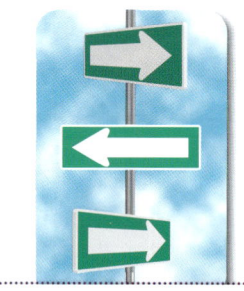

6. It's following the law of the land.

7. It's following what is approved of by society.

8. It's being the kind of person I want to be.

9. It's creating the greatest happiness for the greatest number.

Activities

1. a) Work in pairs. Using a 'Diamond Nine' design, rank the nine statements on page 96 about **being good,** from the one you most agree with to the least. (Design on DVD ROM)
   b) Share your conclusions with another pair. Justify your ranking and if necessary, amend the order of any statements. Decide on your final order and glue your final decisions onto the sheet.
   c) Discuss as a class and then vote on the order.

2. a) Use the glossary and write out the meaning of the following terms:
   - moral
   - immoral
   - amoral.
   b) Read the following statements in the box. Decide whether the actions described are morally good or bad.
   c) Based on these examples, what is it that makes an action morally good?

   i) You deliberately punch your classmate in the arm, knowing it will cause him pain.

   ii) You give half of your packed lunch to your friend who has forgotten hers.

   iii) A teacher puts the whole class in detention because a few pupils will not be quiet when told.

   iv) An evil dictator attempted to poison his enemies with a deadly gas. The attempt failed and scientists discovered that, in fact, the gas provided a cancer cure.

   v) Your mother makes you promise that you will be home by 5.00 pm. On your way home, you discover a woman who has collapsed in the street. You ignore her so that you will be home in time.

3. Think of an example of a person you consider to be morally good.
   a) Explain why you have chosen this person.
   b) What qualities do you admire most about the person's character?

Understand the meaning of Christian morality.
Reflect on what it means for us.

Christian Morality

All Christians share the belief that acting morally means acting in accordance with God's will.

How do we go about discovering God's will for us?

We believe that morality is **revealed** by God. God has, through His relationship with human beings, given certain commands that should govern our behaviour towards Him and each other. To obey these commands is good, and to disobey is evil.

In Judaism, the first five books of the Bible are the Books of Law – these are called the **Torah**. These books contain God's revelation to the Israelites. The Ten Commandments given by God to Moses are the most important.

1. I, the Lord, am your God.

    You shall not have other gods besides me.
2. You shall not take the name of the Lord God in vain.
3. Remember to keep holy the Lord's Day.
4. Honour your father and your mother.
5. You shall not kill.
6. You shall not commit adultery.
7. You shall not steal.
8. You shall not bear false witness.
9. You shall not covet your neighbour's wife.
10. You shall not covet your neighbour's goods.

Activities

1. a) Discuss: imagine that the only rules that existed were the Ten Commandments. Would these be enough by themselves to help us in making moral decisions? Give reasons for your answer.

   b) If you had to make up commandments for the 21st century what would they be?

2. Take the last six of the Ten Commandments (starting with 'You shall not kill') and re-write them in a positive way so that they are commands that state what you **should** do, rather than what you **should not** do.
For example, "You shall not kill" might become, "Treat all forms of life as worthy of respect."

The Greatest Commandment

On one occasion, Jesus was asked: "Which is the greatest commandment?" He replied:

> "You shall love the Lord your God with all your heart, with all your soul, and with all your mind. This is the greatest and first commandment. And a second is like it, you shall love your neighbour as you love yourself. On these two commandments depend all the law and the prophets" (Mt. 22:37-40).

Jesus did not do away with the commandments. He fulfilled them and placed the emphasis firmly on the importance of love:
- an invitation to love,
- a guide on how to love.

Simply not doing wrong is not enough; we must be active in doing good to others. The essential core of the teaching of the Church is God's love for us. Because God loved us first, we are called to reflect God's love for us in our lives and relationships with others.

"Since God has loved us so much, we too should love one another ... God is love and anyone who lives in love, lives in God and God lives in him."[19]

[19] 1 John 4:11,16

Morality based on the God-given desire to love and be loved, involves making the distinction between right and wrong, good and evil. It involves caring for others and reflecting on how our attitudes will affect them. Therefore we are not free to harm another for our own good; nor are we free to ignore the good of others while seeking our own.

Since we are responsible for determining our own behaviour, we must take responsibility for our decisions and actions and the impact these have on the lives of others.

Activities

1. "The commandments do not restrict our freedom but lead to true freedom." Discuss.
   - Say what **you** think and **why**.
   - Give a different point of view and say why some people hold it.
   - Say why you disagree with it.
   - Support your views with examples.

2. Some young people were caught spraying graffiti on public property. They tried to justify their actions by saying:
   It's not harming anyone.
   I'm free to do what I like.
   Others do it.
   a) What do they reveal about their moral values?
   b) What would you want to say to them?

3. In groups of four discuss the scenarios given to you. Imagine you are there.
   a) **Analyse** the range of options open to you.
   b) **Explore** the various consequences of following each option.
   c) **Decide** on the best course of action and justify it.
   d) **Produce** a large mind-map or poster to present a summary to the rest of the class.

   (i) A woman is mugged on a lonely street. As the mugger runs off, some of the contents spill out of the bag – including some money. A young man comes along and helps her to pick up her belongings, unseen by her, he picks up the money.

Activities

(ii) You know that a group of students in your form are writing hurtful things on the internet about others in school.

(iii) Someone in your form is taking illegal drugs. He/she has confided in you and offered you some.

(iv) Your friend wants to spend the night with her boyfriend. She wants you to cover for her and say that she is staying with you.

(v) Your friend has told you that he carries a knife to school. He is scared for his own safety because there are gangs.

(vi) A young man on his first motor bike becomes distracted and knocks down an elderly man on the crossing. There is no one about.

*Consider moral issues we face today.
Reflect on our response to them.*

Current Moral Issues

There are many moral issues facing the world today, such as the growing gap between rich and poor, the misuse of the environment and the many threats to life from conception to old age. On the one hand, we place great value on the gift of life: we rejoice at the birth of a baby and grieve at a death. We put many resources into Health Care to help those who are sick, regardless of their age.

However, in spite of this, violence still threatens life in many forms. Sometimes to make it more palatable or acceptable, we use alternative words such as genocide, holocaust, euthanasia (gentle death or mercy killing) termination, abortion. Abortion is an issue which touches the lives of many young people today.

Abortion – A Serious Moral Issue

The Church's teaching on abortion is clear: human life must be respected and totally protected from the moment of conception. Each human life is sacred: the unborn baby has a right to life.

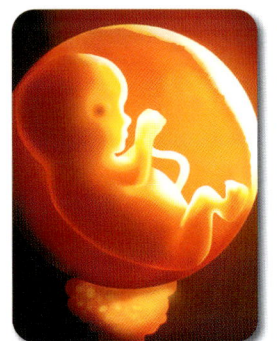

"Human life must be respected and protected absolutely from the moment of conception. From the first moment of his existence, a human being must be recognised as having the rights of a person - among which is the inviolable right of every innocent being to life."[20]

Various reasons have been given in an attempt to justify an abortion: for example, the mother's health, rape or that the unborn baby may be physically disabled. While at times there may appear to be worthy reasons in particular circumstances, Pope John Paul has stated:
"… these reasons and others like them, however serious and tragic, can never justify the deliberate killing of an innocent human being".[21]

[20] Catechism of the Catholic Church, para. 2270
[21] *Evangelium Vitae*, para 58

Pope John Paul II's message to women who have had an abortion:
"The Church is aware of the many factors which may have influenced your decision, and she does not doubt that in many cases it was a painful and shattering decision. The wound in your heart may not yet have healed. Certainly what happened was and remains a terrible wrong. But do not give in to discouragement and do not lose hope … You will come to understand that nothing is definitely lost and you will also be able to ask forgiveness from your child, who is now living in the Lord."[22]

Activities

1. Pope John Paul has pointed out that the **father** of the unborn child, **parents, friends, doctors** and **nurses** may all be guilty of putting pressure on the young person to have an abortion.
   a) Identify the extent to which each of the above may be guilty of the abortion.
   b) Explain how each one could, and should, support a young person who is pregnant.

2. **A nun is approached by a young girl who is pregnant. She says that she can't talk to anyone else. She wants her to take her to an abortion clinic and threatens to commit suicide if she doesn't. The nun is certain that she means it.**
   a) What courses of action are open to the nun?
   b) What do you think she should do? Why?

3. **A young girl discovers that she is pregnant.**
   Identify: 
   a) the courses of action open to her;
   b) the consequence of each course of action;
   c) the line of action you would recommend and why.

[22] *Evangelium Vitae*, para 99

Prejudice and Discrimination

The Universal Declaration of Human Rights declares that all human beings are born free and equal in dignity and rights. They are endowed with reason and conscience and should act towards one another in a spirit of brotherhood. All religions teach that prejudice and discrimination are morally wrong.

Often the words prejudice and discrimination are used interchangeably but in fact they are different.

Prejudice means that we pre-judge, that is we make judgements without prior knowledge.

Discrimination is when we act on those prejudices. So for example, if I am an employer with a prejudice against foreigners, I may take action to avoid employing foreigners in my company. The media can at times foster prejudice and discrimination by stereotyping groups of people such as teenagers, the elderly, immigrants and so forth.

All too often in casual gossip, prejudice and discrimination become intermingled and can destroy peoples lives.

Who Am I?

I maim without killing,
I break hearts and ruin lives. ...
The more I am quoted
the more I am believed. ...
My victims are helpless. ...
To try to track me down is impossible.
The harder you try,
the more elusive I become. ...
I topple governments and wreck marriages.
I make innocent people cry in their pillows.
I am called Gossip.
Office gossip. Shop gossip. Party gossip. ...
Before you repeat a story ask yourself:
Is it true? Is it fair? Is it necessary?
If not – be silent.

      Anonymous

Activities

1. a) Name the TV programme you most frequently watch.
   b) Identify the story lines:
   - betrayal,
   - sincere love,
   - moral uprightness,
   - deceit,
   - generosity,
   - self-sacrifice.

   c) Analyse the influence this programme is likely to have on the lives of young people.
   d) What do you find uplifting about the programme?
   e) Why do you watch it?
   f) What does it tell you about your values?

2. a) Read the 'Parable of the Good Samaritan' (Lk. 10: 29-37).
   b) In what ways is this parable a good example of prejudice and discrimination?
   c) Write your own version of the Good Samaritan in a modern setting.

3. a) Work in pairs. Identify some of the groups that are discriminated against today.
   b) Choose one and explain how pupils in school could act to make a difference.
   c) Share with the class.

4. "Who steals my purse, steals trash,
   'tis something, nothing;
   'twas mine, 'tis his,
   and has been slave to thousands.
   But he that filches from me my name,
   robs me of that which not enriches him
   and makes me poor indeed." William Shakespeare, Othello
   Why is a person's reputation more precious than possessions?

5. Think of a typical week in the life of a teenager today.
   Write a dialogue to illustrate how some of the pressures conflict with living the Beatitudes. (Work sheet TB and DVD ROM)
   It may help to use the idea of the 'good angel' and the 'bad angel' prompting the person to act.

105

Understand what is meant by conscience.
Be aware of how to inform our conscience.

Conscience

1. "There is no pillow so soft as a clear conscience."
   French Proverb

2. "We can believe what we choose; we are answerable for what we choose to believe."
   Blessed John Henry Newman

3. "Conscience is that still, small voice that is sometimes too loud for comfort."
   Bert Murray

4. "In matters of conscience, the law of the majority has no place."
   Mohandas Gandhi

Activities

a) In pairs discuss the meaning of the quotes above.
b) Write your own understanding of each quote.

What is Conscience?

Conscience is the most secret core of our being where we can be alone with God, whose voice echoes within us.

The Church teaches that in the depths of our being, each person detects a law which has not come from ourselves, but which we must obey. This law urges us to love good and avoid evil. It is the voice of **conscience** and, at times, it gives specific guidance such as - do this, avoid that. This law is written in our hearts by God. To obey it is the highest point of honour and we will be judged by it.

> Is conscience like my gut feeling or when I feel a hunch that it's the right thing?

We need to be careful not to deceive ourselves: conscience is much more than a 'hunch' or a 'feeling' about what is right or wrong. It is not a matter of personal preference or opinion. Conscience is not something that allows us to justify doing whatever we want. It is the voice of God resounding in our heart, revealing the truth to us and calling us to do what is good and avoid what is evil.

Conscience does not invent what is right or wrong. It is not our **conscience** that makes the laws. **Conscience is a gift of God**; it is the still, strong, uncomfortable, honest voice inside us that speaks the truth.

Pause
Identify the key points of the Church's teaching on conscience. Use bullet points to list them.

What does the formation of Conscience involve?

The Church teaches that the formation or education of conscience is a lifelong task. If we continually strive to educate it, we will experience peace of mind and heart and the Holy Spirit will guide us.

- **In the formation of conscience, the teaching of Jesus is a light for our path.**
- **A well-formed conscience is upright and truthful.**
- **A well-formed conscience makes judgements in the light of God's Will.**
- **It is important to examine the facts and background about various choices.**
- **The education of conscience guarantees freedom.**
- **It is necessary to reflect on the teaching of Jesus in faith and in prayer and put it into practice.**

Activities

1. Work in pairs. Take one of the statements in the boxes on page 107. Give an example to explain what the statement means.

2. Imagine a good friend is in a difficult situation and has to make a very important moral decision.
State what the moral issue might be and explain how you could help this person in the light of the teaching of the Church.

Erroneous Judgement

We live in an age of moral confusion and relativism, so it is not always easy to recognise the truth. Relativism teaches that each person can make up his or her own truth. For example, it is saying that what is morally right or wrong for me, is not necessarily what is morally right or wrong for you. Another way of putting it is to say, it is right for me because I 'feel' it is right.

Is what our conscience tells us always right?

No, we cannot act just by what we 'feel'. We must always seek what is right and good and discern the will of God.

Rules which will always guide us:
- A person may never do evil so that good will result from it.
- Love your neighbour as yourself.
- Seek seriously what is right and good.
- It is not right to do anything that makes another person sin.

Acting on a misinformed conscience:
A person must always obey the judgement of his or her conscience.
If a person has acted in good faith and taken the necessary steps to inform his or her conscience, then, if the course of action taken is wrong, that person is not guilty.

However, if a person takes little trouble to find out what is true and good or because of habit they ignore that what they are doing is sinful, that person is guilty of the evil committed.

How should we inform our conscience?

The Church teaches that we should carefully
- pray for guidance;
- reflect on the issue in the light of the teaching of Jesus;
- find out what the Catholic Church teaches about it;
- talk to appropriate people about it;
- listen to our conscience;
- wait until we believe we know what God's will is for us.

Activities

1. **"If you believe what you like and reject what you don't like, it is not the Gospel you believe, but yourself."** St. Augustine
   What do you think St. Augustine meant?
   Give two examples to explain the meaning.

2. Imagine you are taking part in a competition for a job which you really want. You are prepared to do whatever it takes to get it (cheat, lie, put others down).
   a) How does the devil try to persuade you that your action is justifiable?
   b) What does the angel tell you to do?

3. **"If someone thinks its right, then it's right for them."** Discuss
   - Say what you **think** about this statement and **why**.
   - Use evidence to support your views from Scripture or the teaching of the Church.

4. **"There is no pillow so soft as a clear conscience."**
   Evaluate this statement in the light of your study on conscience.

5. **"The education of conscience prevents or cures fear, selfishness, pride, guilt and feelings of complacency."**
   a) Analyse this statement.
   b) Give examples demonstrating its relevance.
   c) Show how it is exemplified in the life of St. Thomas More[23] or another person of your choice.

[23] *The Truth*, pp. 116-117

*Know about some people who acted according to their conscience.
Reflect on what we can learn from them.*

Archbishop Romero – The conscience of El Salvador

When Oscar Romero was appointed as San Salvador's Archbishop, he was considered a 'safe' choice, one who would go about his priestly duties and not get involved in politics.

However, Oscar Romero was a person of great integrity. Gradually, he saw what was happening around him, particularly the exploitation and repression of the poor at the hands of the government and the military. Soon, he could keep silent no longer. He became the conscience of the people of El Salvador. He broadcasted weekly on the radio and his homilies called for justice, peace, freedom and forgiveness.

When violence reached his own diocese, his priests were murdered and others received death threats. Archbishop Romero placed the safety of his people before his own. On 23 March 1980, he courageously spoke out for all to hear: "I would like to appeal in a special way to the army's enlisted men. Brothers, you are part of our own people, and yet you kill your brothers and sisters. But before an order to kill that a man may give, God's law must prevail … 'Thou shalt not kill'. No soldier is obliged to obey an order against the law of God. No one has to fulfil an immoral law. It is time to take back your consciences.

The Church, defender of the rights of God, of the law of God, of human dignity, of the person, cannot remain silent before such an abomination. We want the Government to understand. Seriously, these reforms are worth nothing if they are stained with so much blood … In the name of God, and in the name of His suffering people, whose laments rise to Heaven each day more tumultuous, I beg you … I beseech you … I order you in the name of God: stop the repression!"

This was too much for the Government. The following day, Archbishop Romero was assassinated while he was celebrating Mass in his cathedral.

Activities

1. a) Choose three words to sum up Oscar Romero's character.
   b) What arguments did he use to compel others to think seriously about their actions and to follow their conscience?

2. Think of a situation of conflict in some part of the world today.
   Using your own thoughts and those of Oscar Romero, draft an article for a Catholic newspaper urging readers to speak up for the rights of the innocent victims.

When the World looked on, Irena Sendler offered her life …

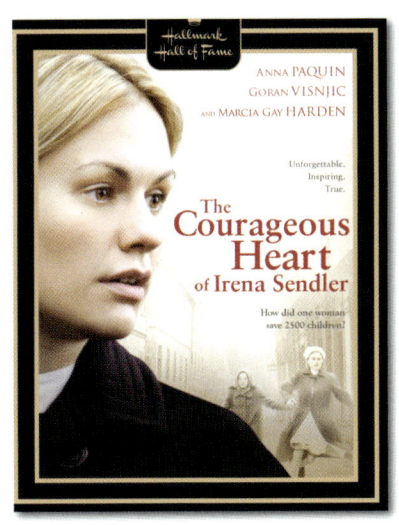

A school history book that briefly mentioned Irena Sendler provoked the interest of four American teenagers. It is thanks to these girls that the world has heard about this brave Polish woman and her heroic struggle to save the lives of 2,500 Jewish children from the Warsaw Ghetto.

In 1939, after the German invasion of Poland, it was forbidden under pain of death to offer help to Jews, but as a committed Catholic, Irena listened to her conscience and lost no time in helping those in need.

A year later, the Germans erected the Warsaw Ghetto and forced 350,000 Jews inside it. It was walled off and guarded. This prevented Irena and her friends helping the Jews. Overcrowded living conditions, dirt, filth and hunger brought sickness and epidemics. The Nazis, afraid of contagious disease, gave permits to some Poles to deliver medicines, offer medical treatments and remove infected Jews. Irena saw her chance!

Irena was a member of Zegota, a secret Polish resistance movement for saving Jews. She managed to obtain forged identification papers to allow her to work as a nurse with the name Jolanta. She lost no time, newborn babies and toddlers were sedated and smuggled out in wooden fruit crates, potato sacks and even in coffins. They were often delivered to the tram driver who drove the vehicle through the Ghetto to the Polish side of Warsaw. Children were smuggled through cellars and sewage canals. There was a church next to the ghetto. Its entrance leading to the ghetto was 'sealed' but if a child could speak Polish and rattle off Christian prayers, he or she could be smuggled through the 'sealed' entrance.

Irena recalls that she had close cooperation from the Catholic Church and she could always count on nuns to take the children into their convents and orphanages. The nuns were poor but they shared what they had and were willing to risk their lives to help.

On a strip of paper, Irena wrote the name of each child as well as the new Polish name given to them. She placed it in a bottle and, at night, buried it under a tree in her neighbour's garden. Every tiny piece of paper was to help the Jewish child find their parents, if they survived the concentration camp.

In 1943, Irena was arrested and tortured by the Gestapo but revealed nothing. She was sentenced to death; taken to the place of execution and urged to run for her life. A member of Zegota had paid a hefty bribe to rescue her.

In 2007, Irena was nominated for the Nobel Peace Prize but it was awarded to Al Gore. A year later, she died at the age of ninety-eight. Not a single child of the 2,500 Irena saved was ever discovered by the Nazis.

Jewish children thanking Irena Sendler.

Activities

1. "Greater love has no man than this, that a man lay down his life for his friends" (Jn. 15:13).
   How is this demonstrated in the life of Irena Sendler?

2. Irena Sendler was nominated for the Nobel Peace Prize but it was awarded to Al Gore, Vice President of the USA in October 2007.
   a) What did Al Gore do to deserve his nomination and award?
   b) How do you think it compares with the work of Irena Sendler?
   c) Who do you think most deserved it? Support your opinion with thoughtful reasons.

A Question of Conscience … Would Jesus pull the switch?

"I was scared out of my mind. I went into the women's toilet because it was the only private place in the death house. I put my head against the tiled wall and grabbed the crucifix around my neck. I said, 'Oh, Jesus God, help me. Don't let him fall apart. If he falls apart, I fall apart'. I had never watched anybody be killed in front of my eyes. I was supposed to be Patrick Sonnier's spiritual adviser.

I was in over my head! All I had agreed to in the beginning was to be a pen pal to this man on Louisiana's death row. Sure, I said, I could write letters. But the man was all alone; he had no one to visit him.

It was like a current in a river, and I got sucked in. The next thing I knew I was saying, 'OK, sure, I'll come to visit you.' He had suggested that on the prison application form for visitors, I filled in 'spiritual adviser', and I said, 'Sure.' He was Catholic and I'm a Catholic nun, so I didn't think much about it; it seemed right.

But I had no idea that at the end, on the evening of the execution, everybody has to leave the death house at 5.45 pm, everybody but the spiritual adviser. The spiritual adviser stays to the end and witnesses the execution.

People ask me all the time, 'What are you, a nun, doing getting involved with these murderers?' You know how people have these stereotypical ideas about nuns: nuns teach; nuns nurse the sick.

I tell people to go back to the Gospel. Look at who Jesus hung out with: lepers, prostitutes, thieves – the throwaways of his day. If we call ourselves Jesus' disciples, we too, have to keep ministering to the marginalised, the throwaways, the lepers of today. And there are no more marginalised, thrown-away, and leprous people in our society than death-row inmates … Jesus Christ, whose way of life I try to follow, refused to meet hate with hate and violence with violence. I pray for the strength to be like him."

Sr. Helen Prejean CSJ

Activities

1. What would Sr. Helen have done before making the difficult decision to support prisoners on death row?
   Try to list six things which would have informed her decision.

2. Did Sr. Helen make the right decision to get involved with Patrick Sonnier?
   a) **Analyse** the range of options open to Sr. Helen as a nun.
   b) **Explore** the various consequences of following each option.
   c) **Evaluate** the meaning and purpose of her mission.

3. Imagine it is the week leading up to the execution of Patrick Sonnier.
   Write a diary account for one of the following:
   • his own mother, or
   • the mother of one of the teenagers he murdered.

*Understand that we are all called to holiness.
Reflect on what this means for you.*

Be Saints not Celebrities

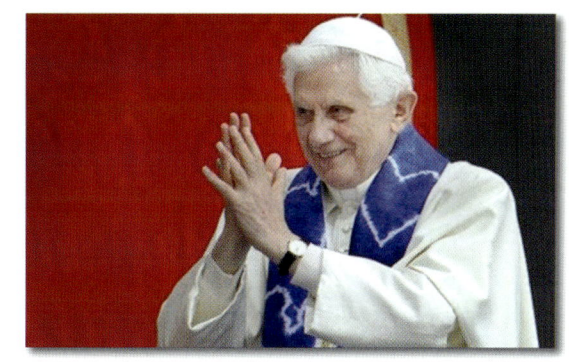

"Fame and fortune do not bring happiness." This was the message Pope Benedict XVI gave to the students of all the Catholic schools of England, Wales and Scotland in September 2010.

"There is something I very much want to say to you. I hope that among those of you listening to me today, there are some of the future saints of the twenty-first century. What God wants most of all for each one of you, is that you should become holy! He loves you much more than you could ever begin to imagine, and He wants the very best for you. And by far the best thing for you is to grow in holiness.

We live in a celebrity culture. Young people are often encouraged to model themselves on figures from the world of sport or entertainment. My question for you is this - what are the qualities you see in others that you would most like to have yourselves? What kind of person would you really like to be?"

Activities

1. What are the qualities you see in others that you would most like to have yourself?
   - Think of some people.
   - Mention their qualities.
   - Say why you would like to have them.

2. a) What are some of the good qualities you have? How do you use them?
   b) What kind of person would you really like to be? Why?

Look for True Happiness

Pope Benedict XVI invites you to become saints. "I am asking you not to be content with second best. I am asking you not to pursue one limited goal and ignore all the others. Having money makes it possible to be generous and to do good in the world, but on its own, it is not enough to make us happy. Being highly skilled in some activity or profession is good, but it will not satisfy us unless we aim for something greater still. It might make us famous, but it will not make us happy. Happiness is something we all want, but one of the great tragedies in this world is that so many people never find it, because they look for it in the wrong places. The key to it is very simple – true happiness is to be found in God. We need to have the courage to place our deepest hopes in God alone, not in money, in a career, in worldly success, or in our relationships with others, **but in God. Only He can satisfy the deepest needs of our hearts.**"

Key to True Happiness

Pope Benedict XVI explains: "Not only does God love us with a depth and an intensity that we can scarcely begin to comprehend, but he invites us to respond to that love. You all know what it is like when you meet someone interesting and attractive, and you want to be that person's friend. You always hope they will find you interesting and attractive, and want to be your friend. God wants your friendship. And once you enter into friendship with God, everything in your life begins to change. As you come to know Him better, you find you want to reflect something of His infinite goodness in your own life.

- You are attracted to the practice of virtue.
- You begin to see greed and selfishness and all the other sins for what they really are, destructive and dangerous tendencies that cause deep suffering and do great damage, and you want to avoid falling into that trap yourself.
- You begin to feel compassion for people in difficulties and you are eager to do something to help them.
- You want to come to the aid of the poor and the hungry.
- You want to comfort the sorrowful.
- You want to be kind and generous.

Once these things begin to matter to you, you are well on the way to becoming saints.

I know that there are many non-Catholics studying in the Catholic schools in Great Britain, and I wish to include all of you in my words…. I hope you too will want to share with everyone you meet the values and insights you have learned through the Christian education you have received."

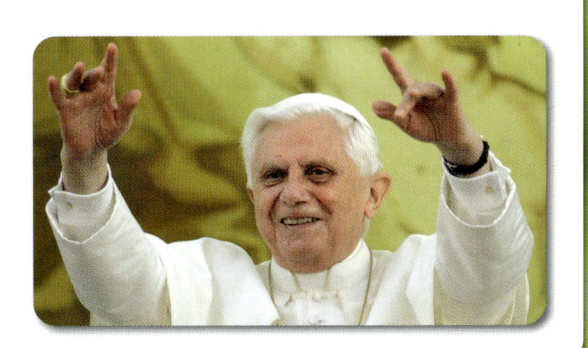

Activities

1. What do you think Pope Benedict XVI means by saying that true happiness is to be found in God?

2. Think about people who are rich and famous in sport or entertainment. Which of them do you think has found true happiness? Give reasons.

3. Think of a time when you have experienced the type of true happiness described by Pope Benedict XVI.
   What was the reason for it?
   How did it feel?
   Were you able to share it? Why or why not?

4. a) Look back through this book; read again the accounts of people who through their relationship with God did something of infinite goodness for others.
   b) Who has been the most inspirational person for you? Why?
   c) Prepare a short presentation on this person to give at a school assembly.

5. When Pope Benedict XVI visited Great Britain in 2010 thousands of people, young and old, greeted him at every stage of his journey. It is reported that over 80,000 attended a Vigil of Prayer with him in Hyde Park, London. Why do you think his visit was so successful? Give five thoughtful reasons.

6. Dialogue with Other Faiths

Know what the Catholic Church teaches about other Faiths. Reflect on the importance of this teaching.

The Catholic Church and other Faiths

The Second Vatican Council, the voice of the Catholic Church world wide, that speaks with the highest authority, defined the relationship between the Catholic Church and other faiths.

In the Vatican II document, *Nostra Aetate*, (In our time), it states:

"All nations are one community and have one origin, because God caused the whole human race to dwell on the face of the earth. They also have one final end, God, whose providence, manifestation of goodness and plans for salvation are extended to all."[24]

Key Issues of *Nostra Aetate*
- The Church rejects nothing that is good and true in other religious faiths.
- The Church encourages dialogue in the search for spiritual and moral values.
- The Church holds that special respect and understanding should be given to the Jews; they are not to be blamed for the death of Jesus Christ.
- All kinds of persecution and discrimination are condemned by the Church.

[24] *Nostra Aetate*, para. 1 (DVD ROM)

"The Catholic Church rejects nothing of those things which are true and holy in these religions. It regards with respect those ways of acting and living and those precepts and teachings which, though often at variance with what it holds and expounds, frequently reflect a ray of truth which enlightens everyone."[25]

Therefore, the Catholic Church recognises that there are **rays of the Truth of God** that can be seen in all people of good will and their religions. These lead them to holiness, even though some of the teaching may not agree with our Christian faith.

The Council calls upon all Catholics to bear witness to the Christian faith and way of life **"to recognise, preserve and promote those spiritual and moral good things"** which are to be found among people of other religions.

Activities

1. a) Study the Key Issues of *Nostra Aetate*.
   b) Number them in the order you think are the most important.
   c) For each Key Issue explain WHY it is important.
   d) Explain what the consequences are likely to be if they are ignored.

   You may wish to use a diagram like this one.

Key Issue	It is important because...	If this key issue is ignored...

2. Think, pair, share.
   The illustration on this page says more than a thousand words.
   a) What is the artist trying to tell us through the use of colour and imagery?
   b) In what ways is it an appropriate image for *Nostra Aetate?*

[25] *Nostra Aetate* para. 2

Lumen Gentium – Light of the Nations

Lumen Gentium, the central document of the Vatican Council on the Church, speaks about our Christian relationship with people of other faiths and none. "God's plan of salvation also includes those who acknowledge the Creator … who with us adore the one merciful God."[26]

Pope Benedict XVI meeting with leaders of other faiths, Assisi, 27 October 2011

Lumen Gentium explains that God wills all people to be saved. He is close to those who seek Him even though they don't know Him. He gives life and breath to all human beings and wills that they should be saved.

The Council affirms that God's grace works through people who seek Him and who, through no fault of their own, do not know the Gospel of Jesus and his Church. Their efforts to seek the truth open them up to the revelation of God in Jesus.

Activities

1. Imagine that you are a Bishop attending the first meeting in your lifetime of a Vatican Council.
   a) What topics will you want to discuss with Bishops from all over the world?
   b) Why do you think good relationships with other faith groups is such a hot topic?

[26] *Lumen Gentium* para. 16

Activities

2. a) Watch the Power Point presentation:
      'Testimonies for Peace' Assisi, 27 October 2011 (DVD ROM).
   b) Reflect on each 'Testimony'.
   c) Write your own testimony.
   d) Work together to create a collective act of worship for 'Peace'.
   e) Seek permission to share it at a school assembly.

Understand the meaning of dialogue.
Reflect on the importance of dialogue with people of other faiths.

Why study other Faiths?

We live in a multi-cultural and multi-faith society. In Britain today, there are Christians from over a hundred different cultures and languages.

We are very likely to meet people of other faiths in a variety of places such as schools, places of work and sports clubs. It is the command of Jesus that we are to treat other people the way we want them to treat us. This is a positive command to love our neighbours.

Our neighbours are Buddhists, Hindus, Jews, Muslims, Sikhs and people of other faiths as well as those who do not recognise God. The documents of Vatican II that we have studied make clear that God loves everyone and we are commanded to love others in the same way.

In this study, we will explore a little about Judaism and Islam. This will help us to go on and look at other faiths later. Judaism, Christianity and Islam all share a clear belief in the one and only God. They all have a special place for Abraham, our 'Father in Faith'.

The Vatican Council has called us to engage in dialogue and to co-operate with the followers of other religions.

Pause to share
How many different nationalities are in your school?
How many people of different faiths do you know?
In what ways are we enriched by knowing people of different cultures and faiths?

Forms of Dialogue

Vatican documents refer to four forms of dialogue.[27]

The dialogue of life

Dialogue literally means 'talking things through'. This can also mean listening to how God works in the lives of others. In this way, we can encourage one another to make the world a better place according to the guidance of God.

Dialogue of life happens when people strive to live as good neighbours. With open hearts, they share one another's joys and sorrows.

Pause
Why do you think it is called the **dialogue of life**?

[27] *Dialogue and Difference*, Christian W. Troll SJ

The dialogue of action

We are all called to 'bear one another's burdens'. We are called to work together against poverty, to promote justice, to look after our world, to stand up for human rights and so establish 'peace in the world'. This can be called the **dialogue of action.**

Pause
What does Jesus say about helping others? Find the answer in Mt. 25: 31-46.

The dialogue of religious experience

If we have a friend of another faith worshipping God in prayer, meditation and pilgrimage, then we have a great deal to share together about our relationship with God.

Religious experience of pilgrimage

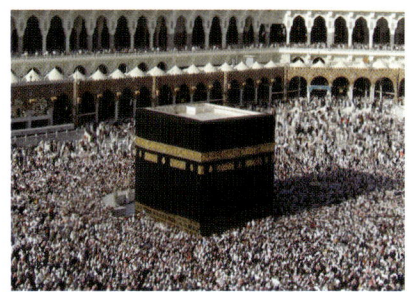

Lourdes

Mecca

This level of sharing religious experience grows slowly and is based on real trust and listening to our hearts as well as our heads. This is the **dialogue of religious experience.**

The dialogue of theological exploration

If I care about you, I will want to know what you think, how you see things, what you believe about God and what He has done in your life and in your faith community. This will help me to understand and appreciate your way of life. This is the **dialogue of theological exploration** and it is where we need the help of specialists.

Pause
Why do you think you are advised to seek the help of specialists?

The importance of dialogue

God is at the centre of our lives and faith. Dialogue is part of this journey of life and faith. As we love and respect God, so we come to love and respect one another.

Through dialogue we grow in understanding, which helps us to understand the position of others with whom we disagree. If I want to be your friend, I owe it to you to find a way to explain clearly my own religious beliefs and practices. Sometimes this is difficult: I may know that something is true and right in my heart but my head has not yet learnt to make sense of it and, sometimes, it is the other way round. Dialogue, like faith, is part of a journey of exploration trusting firmly in God to guide us.

Activities

1. Work in pairs.
   a) To which forms of 'Dialogue' could you contribute? Give examples.
   b) Which form of 'Dialogue' do you think is most important? Give reasons for your answer.
   c) Share your answers with the rest of the class.

2. a) Watch the **Power Point** presentation *The Shoeless Lawyers* (DVD ROM).
   b) Which type of dialogue best fits the mission of Fr. Stanny SJ? Give thoughtful reasons for your answer.

3. Imagine some people have written to the Provincial Superior of the Jesuits to question why one of his priests is helping the Adivasi.
   a) What questions do you think they asked?
   b) Write a reply for the Provincial explaining his reasons. Make reference to the teaching of the Church in *Nostra Aetate*.
   (*The Shoeless Lawyers & Nostra Aetate* DVD ROM)

Fr. Stanny teaching the Adivasi

*Deepen our understanding of Judaism.
Reflect on its importance for us.*

Exploring Judaism

Jesus, a Jew

Jesus was born into a Jewish family. Mary and Joseph were faithful Jews and with Jesus, they followed the Jewish way of life.

When they went to the synagogue on the Sabbath, they took Jesus with them. He was brought up with a deep love, understanding and knowledge of Jewish scriptures, history and tradition. When he was thirteen years old, he became a Bar Mitzvah which meant he was a 'Son of the Commandments'.

The most obvious belief that Jews and Christians share is in God, the one and only God, the creator of everything, who gives and sustains life. God guides human beings and calls us into a relationship based on prayer, worship, family life and ethical living.

Pause to discuss

Why is it important for all Christians to study, understand and respect the Jewish religion?

The Hebrew Bible

God's guidance was sent to the Jewish people in a special way in their scriptures. The most important is the **Torah**, the Law, that is, the five books of Moses.[28]

The **Torah** consists of five books:
- Genesis
- Exodus
- Leviticus
- Numbers
- Deuteronomy.

The Law is an amazing blessing from God. It trains Jews to live according to God's Commandments in every aspect of life. It reminds them who they are and that God has called them to this particular code of ethical living. In this way, Jews are to be a blessing, an inspiration and a witness to all people of their particular Covenant with God.

[28] *The Truth*, p. 38

Inside a synagogue, there is a secure cupboard, often richly decorated, in which are kept the scrolls of the Law.

The Hebrew Bible contains, in addition to the Law, the works of the Prophets and other writings. The Prophets were men and women sent by God to call the Hebrew people back to living according to God's commandments whenever they went astray. This shows us God's desire never to lose contact with any one of His people. Important prophets whose names are in the Hebrew Bible are: Miriam, Deborah, Huldah, Isaiah, Jeremiah and Ezekiel.

Activities

1. Our brains like to have a sense of the complete picture of what we are studying. Make a mind map.
   a) On the thick branches write the names of people you have studied in the Old Testament.[29]
   b) Draw sub-branches and use words or phrases to write the main things you still remember about these people.

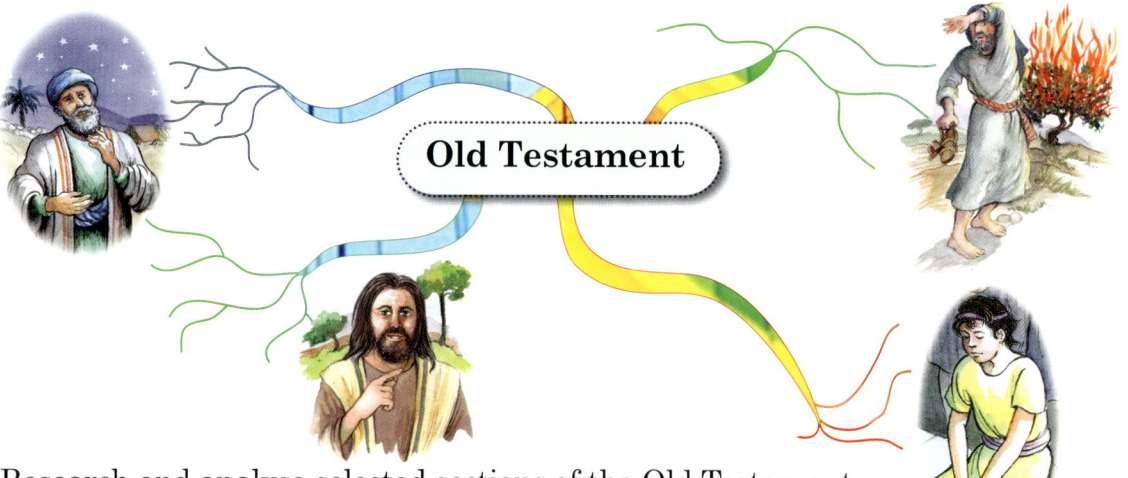

2. Research and analyse selected sections of the Old Testament to show how it can help us today. (WS DVD ROM)

3. a) Research the prophetesses:
      ◦ Miriam
      ◦ Deborah
   b) Which one do you admire most? Why?
   c) What message might she have for us today?
      http://stronginfaith.org/article.php?page=90

4. At the heart of Jewish and Christian worship are the Psalms. Use the worksheet to explore how they can help young people today. (DVD ROM)

[29] *The Way*, pp. 23-26 and The Truth, pp. 42-43

Moral Values

It is in the Hebrew Scriptures that we begin to explore moral guidance about caring for others.

"You shall not wrong a stranger or oppress him, for you were strangers in the land of Egypt. You shall not afflict any widow or orphan…" (Ex. 22:21).

"If you lend money to any of my people with you who is poor, you shall not be to him as a creditor, and you shall not exact interest from him" (Ex. 22:25).

"And when you reap the harvest of your land, you shall not reap your field to its very border, nor shall you gather the gleanings after your harvest; you shall leave them for the poor and for the stranger" (Lev. 23:22).

"If your brother becomes poor and cannot maintain himself with you, you shall maintain him … You shall not lend him your money at interest, nor give him your food for profit" (Lev. 25:35, 37).

"Cease to do evil, learn to do good; seek justice, correct oppression, defend the fatherless, plead for the widow" (Is. 1:16-17).

Activities

1. How did Jesus use the moral guidance of the Hebrew Scriptures? Examples:

   - Mk. 10:19-21
   - Mk. 12:30-31
   - Lk. 4:18-19
   - Lk. 6:20-21

2. What kind of projects might Jews and Christians work on together because of their shared moral values?
   Think about concern for the:
   - environment;
   - disadvantaged and vulnerable in society;
   - land use;
   - business and banking ethics.

3. Work in pairs.
   Imagine one of you is a Jew. You ask your Christian friend to explain the most important Christian beliefs. Role-play the conversation you might have.
   (For help a copy of the Apostles' Creed is on the DVD ROM).

Where Jews and Christians differ

Jews **do not** accept that Jesus is the promised Messiah and truly God. They believe that the Messiah will come at the end of time.

Christians believe that Jesus is the Messiah, truly God and that he will come **again** at the end of time.

Jews recognise Jesus as a very good teacher. While some of his ethical teachings are accepted by them, he does not play a significant part in their religion.

Activities

a) Use the references below to research at least two occasions when there was a strong difference of opinion between some Jewish leaders and the teaching of Jesus.
b) Critically evaluate how these situations were used in different ways by the Jews and by Jesus to provide answers to ethical issues.

Mk. 2:23-28   Jn. 8:3-11   Lk. 11:37-44

Who is Jesus for Christians?

Christians believe that Jesus is the Messiah and the incarnate Word of God.

"At the time appointed by God, the only Son of the Father, the eternal Word, that is, the Word and substantial Image of the Father, became incarnate; without losing his divine nature he has assumed human nature."[30]

Jesus is the Bread of Life sent to us in human form. He is the Saviour of the World, who was crucified and died. Three days later, he rose to eternal life. By his death, Jesus liberated us from sin; by his Resurrection, he opened for us the way to a new life. In short, he is the **Way**, the **Truth** and the **Life**.

Jesus continues to be with us through the sacraments, in the Scriptures and in the people of God, the Church. The following are some of his promises.

---

[30] *Catechism of the Catholic Church*, para 479,

Jesus continues to be with us:
- through the sacraments;
- in the Scriptures;
- in the people of God, the Church.

"I am with you always; yes, to the end of time." (Mt. 28:20)

"Where two or three are gathered together in my name, there am I in the midst of them." (Mt. 18:20)

"If you remain in me and my words remain in you, you may ask what you will and you will get it." (Jn. 15:7)

Activities

1. What evidence is there for the belief that Jesus is divine and human?
   a) Make a chart with two headings: 'Divine' and 'Human'.
   b) Look up the following references and categorise them under the heading of either 'Divine' or 'Human'.

Example:

Divine	Human
	Jn. 4:6 Jesus sat down by the well at Sychar because he was tired.

Mk. 1:32-34   Lk. 2:5-7   Mk. 2:3-12   Mk. 15:37   Mk. 4:35-41

Jn. 11:32-37   Jn. 20:8-10   Jn. 4:6   Jn. 20:19-21

2. a) Research the importance of the observance of the Sabbath for Jews.
   b) Highlight what we can learn from them.

3. Why should we, as Christians, keep Sunday holy?
   Explain in detail the most important ways to do it.

Deepen our understanding of Islam.
Reflect on the importance of recognising and respecting our differences.

✝ Christians and Muslims ☪

Christians and Muslims share the belief that there is one and only one God. This belief is in God who created everything and everyone, God who sustains all living things, God who calls human beings to a life of worship to care for one another and creation and also to ethical living. God guides human beings to the right path and at the end of time, every human being will have to give an account for the way they have lived their life.

Pope John Paul II's vision for young people

Pope John Paul II loved to be in the company of young people. In August 1985, he met with young Muslims in Casablanca, Morocco.

He spoke to them from his heart.

"Christians and Muslims: we have many things in common, as believers and as human beings. We live in the same world.... It is as a believer that I come to you today.

I believe that we, Christians and Muslims, must recognize with joy the religious values that we have in common, and give thanks to God for them. We believe in **one God**, the only God, who is all Justice and all Mercy. We believe in the importance of **prayer**, of **fasting**, of **almsgiving**, of **repentance** and of **pardon**. We believe that God will be a merciful judge to us at the end of time and we hope that, after the resurrection, He will be satisfied with us and we know that we will be satisfied with Him.

Loyalty demands also that we should recognize and respect our differences. Obviously, the most fundamental is the view that we hold on the person and work of Jesus of Nazareth. You know that, for the Christians, this Jesus causes them to enter into an intimate knowledge of the mystery of God and into a filial communion by his gifts, so that they recognize him and proclaim him Lord and Saviour.

Christians and Muslims, in general we have badly understood each other...I believe that, today, God invites us *to change our old practices*. We must respect each other, and also we must stimulate each other in good works on the path of God."[31]

[31] Pope John Paul II's Address to Young Muslims, Morocco, August 1985

Activities

1. Analyse Pope John Paul II's speech to young Muslims. Annotate your own copy of the text. Use two different colours to identify the key points of similarity and difference between Christians and Muslims. (Copy of text DVD ROM).

2. The Pope speaks of Christians entering "into an intimate knowledge of the mystery of God and into a filial communion by His gifts". This is at the heart of our Christian faith, but what does it mean? Explain in your own words. Think about:
   - the sacraments;
   - the Church.[32]

Core Muslim Beliefs

Muslims believe that God is one, unique and unlike any other being or thing. God does not share divinity with any other being or thing. From the beginning of time, God has sent guidance to all the people of the earth. This came through revelations sent down by God; the last of these was the Qur'an.

These revelations were sent to prophets, who were human beings and in no sense divine. They received the guidance from God and put it into practice. They are perfect examples of how to live according to God's guidance. Prophets have been sent to all the people of the earth. The first prophet was Adam, the last was Muhammad. Other prophets mentioned in the Qur'an include Abraham, Moses, David and Jesus.

Human beings were created to worship God, to obey God's commandments and keep away from the things that God forbids. All people are called to respect themselves, one another and the whole creation. We are asked to be just and honest in all our dealings. Each one of us is to remember that we must give an account of our lives on the Day of Judgement.

[32] *The Way* pp. 86-92; *The Truth* pp. 90-91

Activities

1. List what you consider to be the two most important core beliefs in Islam. Give reasons for your choice.

2. Muslims believe that everyone will be weighed in the balance. Our good deeds and our bad deeds will be weighed and we will be rewarded with heaven or hell. However, God is merciful and each good deed will weigh ten times more than each bad deed.[33]

   Find your own way to illustrate this concept.

Muslim Practice

Islam has been likened to a building that stands on five foundations or pillars. These are the five principal practices of Islam. The aim of these is to train people to live a God-centred life; to build up a sense of God-consciousness *(taqwa)*. The one who follows this guidance will be fulfilled in this life and be rewarded by God in paradise.

The Five Pillars of Islam

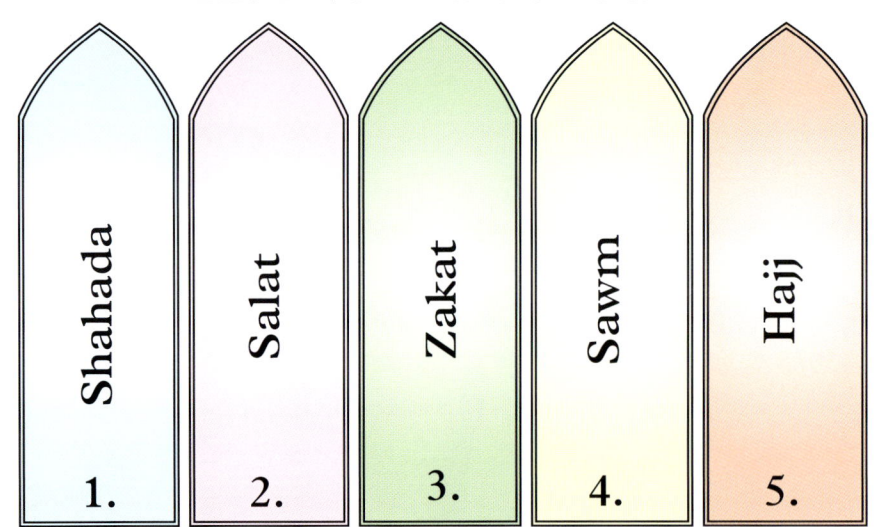

1. Shahada
2. Salat
3. Zakat
4. Sawm
5. Hajj

The five pillars are:
1. *Shahada:* to profess and practise the principal belief of Islam;
2. *Salat:* to pray five times each day;
3. *Zakat:* to purify one's wealth by making money circulate to those who need it;
4. *Sawm:* to fast during the month of Ramadan;
5. *Hajj:* to make the pilgrimage to Mecca once in a lifetime, if health and wealth permit.

[33] Qur'an 17:13-14

Shahada

The shahada states that: "I bear witness that there is no god (that is nothing worthy of worship) save God, Muhammad is the Messenger of God." This is the principal statement of belief for Muslims and they repeat it several times each day and whisper it into the ear of a newborn baby. It is a constant reminder that nothing must get in the way of worshipping, obeying, serving and loving God.

Salat

All adults are required to stop five times each day to offer their formal prayers to God. This prayer takes place at set times and each Muslim wherever they are on earth turns towards the Ka'ba in Mecca to unite as a single community. The sun is always rising and setting somewhere on earth. Therefore every second of every day, this year, throughout the past and into the future the prayer of the Muslim community never stops.

There are never more than a few hours between each formal prayer. This gives Muslims a chance to reflect on their actions and seek God's mercy and forgiveness at the next time of prayer. Verses from the Qur'an are recited during these prayers. They provide guidance for the whole of life.

The five times of Muslim daily prayer

1. Before sunrise
2. After midday
3. Late afternoon
4. Just after sunset
5. At night

Activities

1. What do you think would be the challenges and rewards of this practice of prayer for you?

2. Imagine a Muslim friend asks you about your prayer.
   Take time to think carefully about the answers you might give.
   - Where and when do you pray?
   - How many times daily do you pray?
   - In what language do you pray?

Zakah

The Islamic economic system is based on the principle of 'bearing one another's burdens'. Muslims are only the custodians or stewards of what they own, so all the money they earn, save and spend must be done under the guidance of God.

If another person is in need, then it is their responsibility to try to help. Every year Muslims calculate how much money they have after they have paid for their basic living costs. From this, 2.5% must be made to circulate to those in need. This purifies the remainder of the money but there is no limit to how much more they can freely give in charity.

Pause to discuss
How would you feel about Zakah?
Compare and contrast it with the ways we have of helping the less fortunate?

Sawm

Every Muslim who has reached the age of puberty is required to fast from all food, drink and sexual activities during the daylight hours of the month of Ramadan. Fasting is about self-control. If a person can control their appetites during this month, then they will learn discipline in other aspects of their lives. Ramadan is a month of spiritual stock-taking: Muslims review every aspect of their lives like a spiritual MOT.

Pause to discuss
What are the spiritual and physical benefits of fasting?
When do Catholics fast?

Hajj

Every year approximately two million Muslims, men and women, make the Hajj or pilgrimage to Mecca. This lasts for five days. Muslims of every race, language, culture and social class dress exactly the same to show the equality of humankind. Each day, they perform rituals that are traced back to Abraham, Hagar and Ishmael. On one day, they anticipate the Day of Judgement by seeking the mercy of God. The Hajj includes the Festival of Sacrifice ('Id al-Adha) which recalls Abraham's willingness to sacrifice his son at God's command and the final sacrifice of a ram.

Activities

1. Research: choose one of the following places of Christian pilgrimage.
    - The Holy Land
    - Rome
    - Lourdes
    - Fatima
    - The Way of St. James
    - Walsingham
    - Knock

   Explain:
   - why it is a place of pilgrimage;
   - the variety of reasons why people may go there;
   - the different ways it may help them.

   Use a Power Point or a poster to present your findings.

2. Find out more about Hajj by visiting the website BBC – Religion: Islam Discuss the rewards and challenges of going to Mecca.

Christianity and Islam
Important differences

Christians and Muslims share many key beliefs about God. God is one, unique, indivisible, eternal and all-powerful. God is creator and sustainer of everything that exists. God is transcendent, the essence of God lies beyond our human ability to describe, understand or explain.

Muslims would never speak of God in any way as three; therefore the Christian doctrine of the Trinity has always been a problem for them. No matter how we explain our belief in the one God as revealed in the Trinity, there is always the suspicion and hesitation that this is in some way speaking of three gods or three parts of God. Such a belief would be quite unacceptable to Muslims who stress the absolute oneness of God.

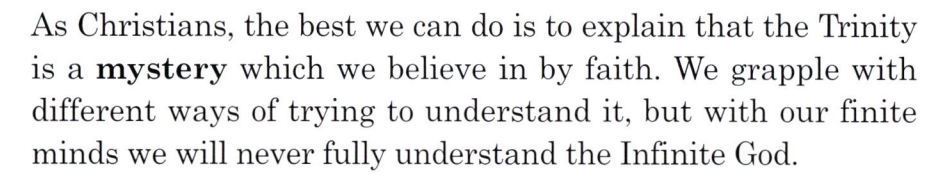

As Christians, the best we can do is to explain that the Trinity is a **mystery** which we believe in by faith. We grapple with different ways of trying to understand it, but with our finite minds we will never fully understand the Infinite God.

Who is Jesus for Muslims?

Muslims have the highest respect for Jesus as one of God's chosen prophets like Abraham, Moses and Muhammad. They believe he received revelations from God and was a sinless, perfect role-model in putting that guidance into practice. He was born of the Virgin Mary and worked miracles by God's permission. He will return to the earth in the Last Days. The Qur'an has a different account of the end of Jesus' earthly life. He was taken up to God before the horrible end of death by crucifixion and he was not resurrected to eternal life.

For us Christians, the all important Death and Resurrection to eternal life of Jesus opens up for us the possibility of sharing in the life of the Risen Jesus now and in heaven.

Muslims do not believe in the incarnation of God in Jesus and will never speak of Jesus as the Son of God. Every Muslim believes that they are capable of living according to God's guidance without the need of a redeemer or saviour. The key Christian belief that Jesus is the Son of God, true God and true Man, Saviour and Redeemer of the world would be quite unacceptable for Muslims.

Activities

1. Imagine a Muslim asks you what you believe about Jesus and why he is important.
   Write your reply. Use some of these scripture references to help you.

   - Mk. 2:5-12
   - Lk. 5:23
   - Lk. 7:48
   - Mk. 14:36
   - Lk. 10:22
   - Jn. 14:6
   - Jn. 14:9
   - Jn. 15:7

2. Christians and Muslims have fundamentally different beliefs about Jesus. Suggest ways in which we could move forward in friendship and co-operation to make the world a better place. Think about the different kinds of dialogue and the message of Pope John Paul II on page 130.

Know how Faith Communities collaborate to help those in need. Consider how we can contribute to the common good of all.

Collaboration of Faith Communities

The declaration on the Church's relation to non-Christian Religions, *Nostra Aetate*, calls upon all Christians to bear witness to the Christian faith whilst co-operating and engaging in dialogue with members of other religions. Together, they should recognise, preserve and promote the common good of all humanity.

Activities

Watch the Power Point presentation:
'Dialogue with other faiths and non-believers', Pope Benedict XVI.
Work in pairs to answer the fifteen questions.

Practical ways of collaborating

The world's greatest movements for change and reform are inspired by people of great faith: people who trust in the power of God to work through them; people who are not afraid to make heroic sacrifices to help the less fortunate. With God's help these people have the courage and enthusiasm to work together to build a better world.

These Non-Governmental Organisations (NGOs) mobilise people of faith to work together on issues of health, education, peace, justice and global poverty. They show the world how to promote unity among faiths by spreading love amongst all.

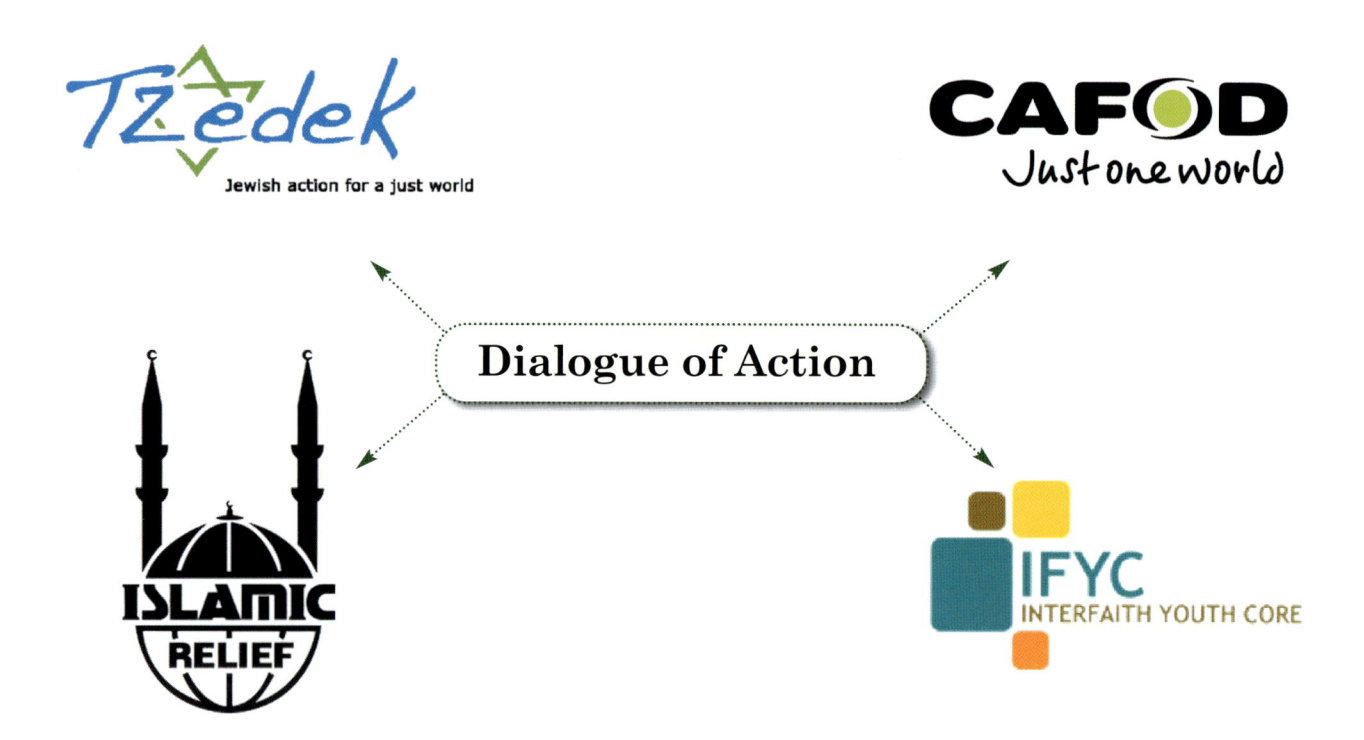

Tzedek — Jewish action for a just world

CAFOD — Just one world

ISLAMIC RELIEF

IFYC — INTERFAITH YOUTH CORE

Dialogue of Action

Jewish action for a just world

Tzedek, Jewish action for a just world works with partners, projects and communities abroad, regardless of their race or religion. It provides direct support to help local people so they can help themselves.

Tzedek is a volunteer-led Non-Governmental Organisation (NGO) that draws upon the skills and resources of the Jewish Community to improve the lives of the less fortunate. It aims to nurture and empower open-minded Jewish community leaders to promote the fight against extreme poverty.

The following is just one example:

Concord Trust 'Cow Bank': TZEDEK initiative

Providing women with a sustainable income, Tamil Nadu, India.

Background: The Concord Trust works in an impoverished part of Tamil Nadu. Very few people own their own land and there are not many jobs available in the region. The best opportunities for employment are only for short periods such as harvest time. This makes earning a living very precarious. People need to find a more regular source of income if they are to lift themselves out of poverty.

The Programme: The programme centres on giving a grant to women to enable them to buy specially selected milk cows. The Concord Trust then arranges training in the care of animals. It also provides insurance for the cow so that if it becomes ill, all the hard work of raising the animal won't be in vain.

The milk produced by the cows provides an additional income that makes an enormous difference to the lives of these families.

Initially, ten cows are provided for ten women. When the cow has its first female calf, it is passed on to another woman. In this way, the number of families with a cow increases over time.

Outcome: 10 cows are provided for 10 women. When these cows have calves, the numbers of beneficiaries will continue to increase over time.

Activities

1. In what ways does the Tzedek initiative enable the people of Tamil Nadu break the cycle of poverty?

2. "The challenge of eradicating disease and poverty should drive us to action not to resignation." Discuss.
   - Say what you think about this statement and why.
   - Quote sources of evidence from the research you have done on Faith Community agencies.

CAFOD
Just one world

CAFOD, the Catholic Agency for Overseas Development, works with all people, regardless of their race, gender, religion or politics; this includes working with aid agencies from other faiths. CAFOD has made a significant commitment to interfaith work by signing an historic Memorandum of Understanding with Islamic Relief Worldwide. Islamic Relief is the largest Muslim aid and development agency based in Britain. It also works with all people regardless of race, gender, religion and politics. The members of CAFOD and Islamic Relief pledge to support each other's joint emergency and development work where circumstances make this possible and appropriate. In addition, they aim to share technical information and resources (such as on water or on HIV), and to strengthen communications on a range of issues.

CAFOD and Islamic Relief work in partnership to help children traumatised by years of violence in Gaza.

Thanks to this agreement, when a massive earthquake struck in Iran, CAFOD was immediately able to send £100,000 to Islamic Relief Worldwide, whose staff worked with the Iranian Red Crescent to provide emergency relief to some of the 70,000 families left homeless in Bam. Another £100,000 was sent to help the victims of flooding in Pakistan and this work continues today.

"What we've achieved through working with CAFOD is a unity of purpose. We have a multi-cultural society not just in the UK but around the world." *(Adel Jaffri, Islamic Relief Worldwide)*

Interfaith Youth Core

There are millions of young people from different faith communities in the world co-operating with each other to make a positive difference. The Interfaith Youth Core builds relationships on the values that we share, such as **hospitality** and caring for the **earth**, and how we can live out those values together.

Aubrey Rose from USA shares her first project when she was fifteen years old:

"We chose landscaping houses on a local not-for-profit project that provides services and housing for the mentally ill. We picked this because we wanted our interfaith group to be about community service that embraces those who feel unwelcome or misunderstood".

Activities

1. Aubrey's mother says: **"Many people think interfaith projects are about proselytizing these young people, but it's really about coming out and saying I'm proud to be a Muslim, a Jew or a Christian. And this is how my faith teaches me to be of service. The point is to share our common values, while celebrating what makes us unique"**.

    Write a reply to Aubrey's mother. Say what you think and try to support your views with good reasons. (More information - worksheet 'Aubrey' DVD ROM).

2. Work in small groups.
    a) Choose one of the four charities on page 138 or another religious charity meeting the needs of the poor and vulnerable.

    b) Visit the charity's website and choose one of its projects. Try to make sure that no other group has chosen the same project.

    c) Prepare a presentation on this project for the class. You must be able to evaluate the project and show that it offers individuals or families the opportunity to rise out of destitution and achieve self-respect.

    d) As a class, decide on which project you believe to be the most in need of help. Decide on a way to raise some funds to make a donation to it.

Glossary

Absolution	being freed from guilt; complete forgiveness of sins
Allegory	description of one subject using another, similar subject (e.g. in Bunyan's *A Pilgrim's Progress,* a journey is used to represent life)
Amoral	an action that has no moral value; it is morally neutral and could not be described as good or bad
Apostle	'one sent out' to preach the good news
Apostolic religious life	the way of life of monks and nuns who are called to serve God by working in the world (e.g. in schools or hospitals)
Beatitudes	eight sayings, at the heart of Jesus' teaching, about true happiness with God
Blessed Sacrament	the real presence of Jesus in the form of consecrated bread
Charism	a special spiritual gift
Commissioned	to be entrusted with a task
Conception	the beginning of a new human life; fertilisation
Conferred	granted to someone
Conscience	our inner voice that tells us right from wrong
Discernment	the prayerful process of discovering God's will for your life
Disciple	'learner or follower'; the disciples followed Jesus during his ministry on earth in order to learn from him
Divine Office	psalms and prayers said (and sung) daily by members of the Church
Ecclesiastical law	rules laid down by the Church
Indelible mark	a mark that cannot be removed
Immoral	actions that are contrary to an established rule or principle
Initiation	bringing into membership of a group
Magi	wise men from the East skilled in the study of the stars

Messiah	also known as the Christ; the leader longed for by the people of Israel; a Hebrew word meaning 'anointed one by God' and consecrated to Him.
Metaphorical language	use of a name or descriptive phrase applied imaginatively to an object or action (e.g. food for thought; to leave no stone unturned)
Monastic	characteristic of monks or nuns
Monstrance	a vessel in which the Blessed Sacrament is shown for adoration
Moral	it comes from the Latin *moralis* and is concerned with the distinction between right and wrong (e.g. in behaviour)
Natural law	'the original moral sense'; it enables humankind to distinguish, by reason, the difference between good and evil
Novitiate	the part of the convent or monastery where novices live
Philosopher	a lover of wisdom; a student of the science of being and knowing
Professing our faith	freely acknowledging our belief in God
Rabbi	a Jewish doctor/teacher of law
Renounce	to give up; abandon (e.g. a habit, practice, belief)
Retreat	a period of quiet seclusion enabling us to reflect on God and our life
Salvation	being saved, being completely close to God
Secular humanists	students of human affairs or of human nature in this world only
Supreme	above everything; highest authority or rank
Tabernacle	a special, secure container, usually on or near an altar, in which the Blessed Sacrament is reserved.
Theologian	one who studies the nature of God and his relations with humankind and the universe
Vocation	calling from God
Wake	a ceremony when family and friends watch over the body of a deceased person before burial

Acknowledgments

Second and new edition: May 2012

A joint enterprise by:
Teachers' Enterprise in Religious Education Co. Ltd and Sr Marcellina Cooney CP

Nihil obstat: Father Anton Cowan – Censor.

Imprimatur: The Most Reverend Vincent Nichols PhL, MA, Med, STL
Archbishop of Westminster
21 April 2012, Feast of St. Anselm, Bishop & Doctor.

The *Nihil obstat* and *Imprimatur* are a declaration that the books and contents of the DVD ROM are free from doctrinal or moral error. It is not implied that those who have granted the *Nihil obstat* and the *Imprimatur* agree with the contents, opinions or statements expressed.

Theological Advisor: Fr Herbert Alphonso SJ

Picture Research: Sr Marcellina Cooney CP & Ian Curtis

© 2012 Sr Marcellina Cooney CP – Design & Text

© 2012 Ian Curtis, First Sight Graphics – Design, Compilation & Format

© 2012 Jenny Williams; Philip Hood, Arena Illustrations

Copyright notice
All rights reserved. No part of this publication may be reproduced in any form or by any means (including photocopying or storing it in any medium by electronic means without the written permission from the Teachers' Enterprise in Religious Education Co. Ltd)

Acknowledgements
Considerable thanks are due to the head teachers of the following schools for making it possible for their teachers to attend Editorial Meetings: Blessed George Napier, Banbury OX16; Hagley High, Stourbridge DY8; Ilford Ursuline High, IG1; John Henry Newman, Stevenage SG1; St. Joseph's, Croyden SE19; Ursuline, Kent 8LX
Grateful thanks are also due to the many people who helped with proof reading the text.

Permission credits
Cover photos: stained glass window © CWS Design, 9 Ferguson Drive, Lisburn BT28 2EX; sea © Sr. Marcellina Cooney CP. Page 4 illustration by Elizabeth Wang, T-06628-CW, © Radiant Light, www.radiantlight.org.uk. Page 7 & 119 illustrations by Elizabeth Wang, T-07009C-CW, T-01269-OL © Radiant Light, www.radiantlight.org.uk; Pages 9, 48, 64, 103 photos © Sr. Marcellina Cooney CP. Pages 11, 13, 47, 98 stained glass windows from St. Luke's Catholic Church, Dunmury, Belfast BT17 Diocese of Down & Connor, used with permission from Rev. Brian McCann PP. Pages 13 & 14 stained glass windows of the Trinity from Holy Family Catholic Church, Belfast BT15, used with permission of V. Rev. Gerard McCloskey. Pages 17, 35, 39, 40, 44, 45, 46, & 50 © ITV Global Entertainment. Page 17 photo of Cardinal Hume by Bill Gribbin, courtesy of Westminster Cathedral Archives. Page 18 photo © Columban Sisters, Peru; photo of children, © Mary's Meals. Pages 22 & 23 Last Judgement, Michelangelo, © AKG Images; clip art © Mille Images d'Evangile by Jean-François Kieffer. Page 25 clip art © Milles Images Symboliques by Patrick Royer. Page 27 photo of Dorothy Day © Department of Special Collections & University Archives, Marquette University WI 53201-3141. Page 31 J. Jordaens, Four Evangelists © AKG Images. Page 33 Caravaggio, Inspiration of Matthew, © AKG Images. Pages © ITV Global Entertainment. Page 36 Borovikovsky, Mark the Evangelist, © AKG Images. Page 41 Luke the Evangelist, Collectors Card, © AKG Images. Page 46 St. John the Evangelist, Reni, Guido © Bridgeman Art Library. Pages 47 & 65 clip art image Religious Clip Art © McCrimmon Publishing Co. Ltd www.mccrimmons.com/info@www.mccrimmons.com Publishing. Pages 52, 54 & 55 photos from St. Aloysius Catholic Church, London NW1, used with permission of Fr. James McNichols. Page 58 used with permission of the Jane Tomlinson Appeal. Page 68 clip art image, Signs Symbols & Saints, © McCrimmon Publishing Co. Ltd www.mccrimmons.com/info@www.mccrimmons.com Publishing; photos 68, 69, 70, 122, 123 &124 Jesuits Year Books 2005 & 2011 used with permission of Giuseppe Bellucci SJ. Pages 71 & 72 Jesuits Year Book 2007 used with permission of Giuseppe Bellucci SJ. Page 77 © Let the Children Live. Page 78 illustration T-00070-BW by Elizabeth Wang, © Radiant Light, www.radiantlight.org.uk. Page 79 photo © K & E Scott. Page 82 © Andras Simon and McCrimmon Publishing Co. Ltd. Pages photos 80, 83, 84 & 85 © Ian Curtis. Page 86 © Sr. Mary Stephen CRSS and McCrimmon Publishing Co. Ltd www.mccrimmons.com/info@www.mccrimmons.com Page 87 stained glass window © CWS design; the illustration is by Elizabeth Wang © Radiant Light. Photos pages 89 & 90 © Society of Jesus, UK . Page 92 used with permission of Sr. Alicia Pérez FCJ. Page 94 photos © Poor Clares, Arundel & Brighton; page 95 stained glass windows © Passionists Fathers. Photo page 110 is used with permission of the Archbishop Romero Trust. Pages 111 & 113 photos of Irena Sendler © Yad Vashem, Holocaust Martyrs' Heroes' Remembrance Authority, Jerusalem & photos from film 'The Courageous Heart of Irena Sendler' © Hallmaark Hall of Fame and used with permission. Page 113 & 114 photos © Sr. Helen Prejean. Page 118 photo © Felici Fotografia, Rome. Pages 120 & 121 © L' Osservatore Romano Fotografia, Rome. Page 133 photos of nature © Sr. Marcellina Cooney CP. Page 139 photo © TZEDEK; page 149 photo © CAFOD; page 141 photo © Aubrey Rose. All the following used throught and courtesy of Shutterstock.com, © Elenamiv, © Bocos Benedict, © Howard Sandler, © Joel Calheiros, © JonasDalidd, © jon le-bon, © Yanik Chauvin, © KSR, © Antony McAulay, © RTimages, © ayazad, © Rick Becker-Leckrone, © Indigo Fish, © Nicemonkey, © Vladimir Melnik, © Anton Albert, © Sorin Popa, © Rahhal, © wrangler, © Propovednik, © imageoptimist, © linerpics, © Tatiana Serkova, © Faniell, © Adam Fraise, © Warren Price Photography, © Andresr, © -Albachiaraa-, © Alexander Smulskiy, © iodrakon, © vector-RGB, © getvitamin, © antishock, © Lasse Kristensen, © Joachim Wendler, © Mark Beckwith, © Konstantnin, © CREATISTA, © Norph, © Warren Goldswain, © sagasan, © neff, © graph, © val lawless, © MitarArt, © biletskiy, © casejustin, © Meryll, © Itana, © koya979, © Milos Jaric, © Rechitan Sorin, © Christopher Jones, © Yuri Arcurs, © stavklem, © William Perugini, © Tamara Kulikova, © Elena Elisseeva, © Pavel Lysenko, © Monkey Business Images, © VikaSuh, © Petr Vaclavek, © atm2003, © konstantynov, © Complot, © STILLFX, © Lightspring, © PaintDoor, © Dmitriy Shironosov, © SuriyaPhoto, © silver tiger, © Tancha, © AlexSmith, © mathom, © Mikael Damkier, © Sheftsoff, © Robert Hoetink, © Leah-Anne Thompson, © alessandro0770, © mkabakov, © Helga Pataki, © Robert Kneschke, © Hasloo Group Production Studio, © Melica, © Anthony Correia, © samarttiw, © Prapann, © echo3005, © SnowWhiteimages.

Every effort has been made to contact copyright holders of material used in this publication. Any omissions will be rectified in subsequent printing if notice is given to the Teachers' Enterprise in Religious Education, Co. Ltd, 40 Duncan Terrace, London N1 8AL

Published by
Teachers' Enterprise in Religious Education Co Ltd
40 Duncan Terrace, London N1 8AL

Printed in the UK by Geerings Print Ltd, www.geeringsprint.co.uk